TEXAS
Ukulele

TEXAS
Ukulele

The Plucky History of a Hawaiian
Instrument in the Lone Star State

JEFF CAMPBELL

THE
History
PRESS

Published by The History Press
Charleston, SC
www.historypress.com

First published 2025

Opposite: Roy Wood with his ukulele collection. *Photograph courtesy of Dallas Ukulele Headquarters.*

Manufactured in the United States

ISBN 9781467156844

Library of Congress Control Number: 2024945421

Dedication
Uncle Roy

This book is dedicated to my friend and mentor, Roy "Uncle Roy" Wood (1934–2024). Roy taught me a lot, and if I'm honest, he taught me more about life than about music. This is Roy's story.

In Hawaiian culture, it is common to refer to your elders as uncle or aunty as a sign of respect. No one in the North Texas ukulele community is more respected than Roy Wood.

If you have ever attended a ukulele jam in the area, it's likely you have heard the following conversation (or something similar): "Hey, that's a nice ukulele! Where did you get it?" "Roy gave it to me." Fondly referred to as Uncle Roy, Roy Wood has given away hundreds of ukuleles over the years. "I stopped counting a while back when I reached one hundred. Christmas of 2021, I gave twenty-two ukuleles to Stults Elementary."

How did Uncle Roy become the philanthropist of the four-string?

It was June of 2010, after my wife died, and I suddenly found myself alone and needing something to occupy my time. I took the little ukulele that was hanging on my wall and never played and went onto the internet and found the Dallas Ukulele Headquarters, which subsequently became my second family. At the time I joined DUH, the membership was about three hundred and is now 1,800 locally, nationally and internationally.

Soon, I bought a baritone ukulele, which is the largest of the four standard sizes of the ukulele, and with four others formed the Baritone Ukulele Group (BUGS). One of the group members was Jim Mills, who was to become a resident of PVN. Jean Mills, Jim's wife of sixty-six years, was a resident of the memory unit at Signature Place, where two of the DUH members performed at Jim's request, and it was my first experience witnessing the response of such residents to music.

People who seemed to have little or no response to their surroundings would tap a foot or pat a leg. Some would hum or nod their head in time to the music. Jim is no longer with us, but my visits with him here at PVN strongly influenced my decision to make this my home.

DUH and BUGS have played at several retirement and nursing homes, Dallas Heritage Village at Christmas, Dallas Zoo and other venues. The ukulele continues to fill my lonely hours. I sometimes play at 3:00 or 4:00 a.m. and thankfully do not disturb my neighbors. I am also thankful for the PUPS (PVN Ukulele Players); they make my life meaningful, and we rejoice in sharing our music with others. We have performed at Happy Hour, Village Council Meeting, Grey Fox Follies and celebrated Christmas in all of the residential halls.

In my humble opinion, two of the essentials in life are a sense of humor and a ukulele. You need to be able to laugh at yourself, and playing the ukulele or other musical instrument will take a lot of stress out of your life. So, if you want to learn how to play the ukulele, I give free lessons and furnish the uke. Just don't ask me to play "Tiptoe Thru the Tulips" like Tiny Tim!

—Roy Wood

ROY PLAYED CLARINET AND saxophone in high school. He graduated in 1951 at the age of sixteen and attended Midwestern University on a band scholarship. He was a member of the Official Governor's Band State of Texas from 1951 to 1953. "Early on, I believe that music is important in people's lives, and the ukulele is almost a universal instrument," he said.

Uncle Roy can teach a person a lot about playing the ukulele: how to tune it, how to strum it and how to play all of the chords. However, the best lesson Uncle Roy can teach someone is to be a giving person and pay it forward, not only with his time, but also in giving away ukuleles.

Musician Linda Lasseter has played with Roy for many years, "Roy became a friend when he gave me a Bruce Wei tenor. I had bought a baritone, but it was not a fine instrument; I later gave it to my girlfriend in Atlanta. I admire Roy's dedication to inspiring so many others to play the ukulele. He has given away many good quality ukes, plus changed strings on many more. He's done lots of classes and private lessons—all free."

Mark Levine of Dallas Ukulele Headquarters is another person who has been very close to Roy.

Roy Wood started his involvement with Dallas Ukulele Headquarters after his wife died. I honestly don't know how closely those events followed each other, but he's become a huge part of the ukulele family. If I remember correctly, he originally formed a baritone group to provide support to baritone players, which initially met at his house and eventually became the BUGS group. Again, my details of the origin story are unclear. It may be

Roy Wood teaches a beginner ukulele class at the Richardson, Texas Senior Center. *Photograph from the Jeff Campbell collection.*

Bob and Judy Sparkman were always in charge, but it was just held at Roy's house. I remember practicing many of our Ebby Halliday birthday performances at his house. We also built Wolfelele ukuleles at his house. I still have a special one he engraved a special drawing on the back of. He even had my wife and I move in when we were looking for a house, along with our two little dogs! He has provided uncountable hours of training, musical expertise, support, caring and involvement. Our current amplification system was purchased and donated by him and about a gazillion ukuleles. He doesn't do it these days, but Roy used to buy ukuleles all the time and generously donate them to just about anyone who might benefit. We've used many as prizes for fundraisers. There's likely a large chunk of DUH members strumming along on ukes that Roy had purchased. Much of what Dallas Ukulele Headquarters has accomplished since he joined has been influenced and improved by his contributions.

Roy Wood and Jeff Campbell warming up their conch shell skills. Conch shells are blown before every Kanikapila gathering. *Photograph from the Jeff Campbell collection.*

A memorial ukulele celebration was held for Roy at Guitars & Growlers in Richardson, Texas on August 17, 2024. It would have been Roy's ninetieth birthday.

Aloha Texas

Aloha in Texas is a big howdy, we ain't got beaches like in Wai-ki-ki
But we're big sky friendly and we want you to know,
You can still spread a blanket at the Gulf of Mexico
Grab your Hawaiian shirt and ten-gallon hat, grass skirt and coconuts,
    cowboy boots and chaps
Wear almost anything and still get a date, aloha from the Lone Star State

We like our honky-tonks and western swing, three long necks later we
    like just about anything
Willie and Waylon, steel guitar and dobro, but after midnight we'll do
    the hula with Don Ho
Orchids and lilies, they're alright, I suppose, but we still love our San
    Antonio Rose
We'll teach you to two-step, hula till it's late, aloha from the Lone Star State

Smokin' volcanoes, that's the one thing we ain't got,
But our Texas campfire chili burns just as hot
Our barbeque and ribs are the best you've ever tried,
and when we want some fish, you know it's got to be deep fried

We like to party when the sun goes down, barbeque a pig but we don't
    put it in the ground
Bring your ukulele and your slack key guitar, we will throw in twin
    fiddles and be swingin' on a star
Romance your baby in the Lone Star way, you might be in Texas but
    you can still get a lei
Hawaii and Texas, there's no need to bifurcate, aloha from the Lone
    Star State
Hey ya'll and howdy, aloha from the Lone Star State
We really mean it, aloha from the Lone Star S-t-a-t-e

Written by Dirje Childs, John B. Smith & David Hendley
© copyright Buddha Frau Musik, ASCAP & Farmpots Music, ASCAP[1]

Contents

Foreword

When my friend Jeff Campbell first told me about the book he was writing on Texas ukulele history, I was a bit skeptical. After all, how much content could you write about this Hawaiian instrument, especially within the Lone Star State?

As I started reading it though, a few things became immediately apparent. For one, there's so much more to the uke than I could've ever imagined. You see, I'm not a ukulele player, and I definitely haven't dug into the instrument's origins. Ironically, I'm a musician who plays something that is often mistaken for the ukulele, the mandolin. Many other mandolinists and I have found ourselves having to explain time and time again the differences between the two small instruments. Because of this, I drew some ill-informed conclusions and judgments about the ukulele. I thought it was just a simple little instrument that required minimal effort to play.

While the instrument does have an element of simplicity, there's a wealth of creativity and exploration that can be found. Players such as Kevin Carroll, Cas Haley and even Peter Rowan, who's primarily known for bluegrass music, have taken the ukulele to greater heights. There's a true level of artistry that I have immense respect for now.

Another realization this book brought to me is the strong sense of community the ukulele has provided. Groups such as the Dallas Ukulele Headquarters, the Kanikapila Island Strummers and numerous others have brought people together, not only to share their love for the instrument

Right: Author, historian, musician and writer Braeden Paul. *Photograph from the Braeden Paul collection.*

Below: The author and Braeden Paul signing copies of their book *Texas Bluegrass Legacies* at the Bloomin' Bluegrass Festival in Farmers Branch, Texas. *Photograph from the Jeff Campbell collection.*

but also to pass on knowledge and keep the uke played and enjoyed for generations to come.

Among other things, *Texas Ukulele* has made me want to get a baritone uke of my own (much to my family's dismay)! Get ready to say "Aloha" to the journey that Jeff is taking you on with this wonderful book.

—Braeden Paul

Braeden Paul is a music critic, historian and musician. As a mandolinist, he has performed with multiple Dallas-based bands and has appeared as a guest instrumentalist with Grammy Award winner Michael Cleveland.

Braeden has contributed numerous music reviews to both Bluegrass Today *and the* Bluegrass Society of America. *He also coauthored* Texas Bluegrass History *(The History Press, 2021) and* Texas Bluegrass Legacies *(The History Press, 2023) with Jeff Campbell.*

Braeden currently serves on the board of directors of both the Southwest Bluegrass Club and the Garland Square Pickers. He's also the founder of Braeden Paul's Bluegrass Preservation, a YouTube channel that contains rare video and audio recordings of bluegrass and other forms of traditional acoustic music.

Preface

One holiday season, many years ago, my wife and I were shopping in our local bookstore. As we made our way to the register with our bundle of books, we spotted a plastic ukulele. Looking at each other, we both nodded yes and laughed. At the minimum, it would be a whimsical decoration under our Christmas tree.

One morning, motivated by my second cup of Tim Hortons coffee, I tried to play the ukulele. It sounded terrible. Using an app on my phone, I was able to tune the ukulele. However, it did not stay in tune for very long. Realization quickly set in that this plastic ukulele was no more than a child's toy. So, now we're off to Amazon to order a real ukulele. The determined will not be deterred.

First, let's take time out for an author's confession. Up until this time, my musical history was limited to trying to play trombone in sixth grade (I could never play anything more than B flat, which seemed to anger my teacher immensely) and playing a little electric bass in my late teen years. Nevertheless, I had ukulele fever and was excited about this new adventure.

I started learning with Robert Krout at Southern Methodist University. At the end of our semester, Robert announced he was relocating to Galveston. Where do I go from here? A quick Google search revealed a subculture I did not know existed.

I began playing with Joe Stobaugh at the Frisco Ukulele Society and Grace Avenue Ukes. There were workshops and jams to attend sponsored by the Dallas Ukulele Headquarters, which, in turn, introduced me to the

Above: The author (*left*), Maria Victoria McElroy (*center*) and Obed Donlin (*right*) lead a song at Kanikapila in Carrollton, Texas. *Photograph from the Jeff Campbell collection.*

Left: The author jamming with a friend. *Photograph from the Jeff Campbell collection.*

monthly Kanikapila held in Carrolton, Texas. Other group jams included those with the Baritone Ukulele Group (BUGs) in Addison, Texas, and the Fort Worth Ukulele Group.

The COVID era slowed us all down, but our friends in Austin came to the rescue. I was able to study Celtic ukulele with Kevin Carrol on Zoom, and the Austin Ukulele Society started posting their meetings on YouTube.

Through the years, I have had the opportunity to perform with the Chordbusters Ukulele Band, Opihi Gang Hawaiian Band, East Dallas Uke-A-Ladies at Uke a Palooza, the DUH Christmas Band, the Dukes of Ukes & Uke-A-Ladies and the "Fat Sunday" Mardi Gras celebration in Fort Worth.

As I have traveled across Texas with this little four-string strummer, I have met many wonderful people. I hope to introduce you to them and many other fascinating ukulele musicians in this book.

—Jeff Campbell

Thanks, Mark Levine!

I t would have been impossible for me to complete this project without the help of Mark Levine. Mark is the founder and head honcho of Dallas Ukulele Headquarters (DUH). Mark is not only a skilled ukulele teacher and performer, but he is also a ukulele encyclopedia.

As a teacher, he is patient and encouraging to beginners that come to the DUH jams. His timing and comedic skills make him the perfect leader of the DUH Community Ukulele Band.

Whenever I had a question about an event, group, band or individual, Mark was quick with an answer. It seems like he knows everybody and everything about ukuleles, especially in Texas. In this book, you will read more about Mark and Dallas Ukulele Headquarters. Also throughout this book, Mark shares his thoughts on the various people and groups that make up the Texas ukulele community.

Thanks, Mark!

—Jeff Campbell

Mark Levine leads the Dallas Ukulele Headquarters Community Ukulele Band in Christmas rehearsals in 2018. *Photograph courtesy of Dallas Ukulele Headquarters.*

Acknowledgements

I sometimes get comments like, "You wrote this yourself?" The answer is yes, I did write it, but I did not write it by myself.

I want to thank Braeden Paul for writing the foreword to this book. Braeden also did the first edit of the contents, and I am grateful.

Mahalo to my ukulele family of Roy Wood, Richard Muir, Obid Donlin, Mark Levine, Joe Stobaugh and Linda Lasseter for their encouragement, guidance and opportunities.

Mark Miner operates the website Minerd.com, a biographical archive of early Pennsylvania German families. Without Mark, the Bobby Henshaw story in this book would have never happened. Thanks, Mark!

Dallas Ukulele Headquarters! Thank you for access to your vast archive of photographs. A lot of great moments and a few wonderful memories for me.

Thanks to The History Press and Arcadia Publishing for heading out on another adventure with me! This is our eighth project together.

As I was researching this project, I ran across a wonderful piece written by Barbara Haefeli. Barbara wrote about navigating the pandemic era better than I ever could. She also paid tribute to a Texas ukulele icon, Kevin Jolly. I am deeply appreciative that Barbara allowed me to share it in this book.

To all of the musicians, from the Piney Woods to the Llano Estacado, thank you for taking the time to discuss Texas and ukuleles.

Thanks to all of the groups I have been able to play with over the years, including the Frisco Ukulele Society, the Grace Avenue Ukulele Choir, the

Left: The Chordbusters Ukulele Band performs at Morada Senior Living in Arlington, Texas. *Photograph from the Jeff Campbell collection.*

Right: The Chordbusters bandleader, Doris Whitlock. *Photograph courtesy of Pat Dodson Douty and the Chordbusters Ukulele Band.*

Suncreek Strummers, the East Dallas Uke-A-Ladies, the Kanikapila Island Strummers, the First Congo Ukers, the Baritone Ukulele Group, the Opihi Gang, the Austin Ukulele Society, the Dukes of Ukes & Uke A Ladies, Southern Methodist University Continuing Education and whatever the Fort Worth ukulele group is calling themselves these days.

Winding this up, I want to thank my band, The Chordbusters Ukulele Band of Arlington, Texas. The Chordbusters have been around since the early 1990s. Every Wednesday, except holiday weeks, the Chordbusters perform at a rotating group of assisted living facilities, retirement facilities and memory care centers. The Chordbusters bring a lot of "ukulele joy" to the community. I am proud to be a part of this band!

1

Texas Instruments

Let's talk about Texas instruments. No, not the information tech company founded in Dallas. Let's talk about Texas musical instruments.

The first thing that comes to mind is the guitar. The guitar is synonymous with the Lone Star State, from the famous guitars, like Willie Nelson's Trigger; Buck Owens's red, white and blue special; and Stevie Ray Vaughan's Number One, to those owned by the local strummer. In Texas, it's not a state law that every home should have a guitar inside; it just seems that way.

Another instrument with strong roots in Texas is the fiddle. This is due in large part to the legendary Bob Wills (1905–1975). Wills created a new genre of American music, western swing.

> *I grew up on music*
> *That we call western swing*
> *It don't matter who's in Austin*
> *Bob Wills is still the king*
> *—Waylon Jennings*

The Texas fiddle tradition continues with fiddle contests across the state. By the way, do you know the difference between a fiddle and violin? It's a violin if you're selling it. It's a fiddle if you're buying it.

Texas also has a rich accordion culture, a true gumbo of Cajun, Zydeco, German and Tejano styles and influences. If you have time, check out the

Left: The author with Buck Owens's famous red, white and blue guitar at the Sherman Museum in Sherman, Texas. Buck was born in Sherman in 1929 and donated the guitar to the museum. Notice the gloves to protect this historical artifact. *Photograph from the Jeff Campbell collection.*

Right: Becky Buller playing fiddle at the 2017 Wylie Bluegrass Festival in Wylie, Texas. *Photograph from the Jeff Campbell collection.*

Big Squeeze accordion contest and the Accordion Kings & Queens concert from Texas Folklife.

In addition, piano maestro Van Cliburn (1934–2013) brought worldwide acclaim to Texas. Van Cliburn wowed music lovers from Carnegie Hall to Moscow. The Van Cliburn International Piano Competition has been held in Fort Worth, Texas, since 1962. Every four years, The Cliburn brings the best pianists in the world to Cowtown.

But what about the ukulele? People think Hawaii—not Texas—when you mention the ukulele. However, there is over one hundred years of Texas ukulele history. Let's explore the untold tales of the smallest stringed instrument in the biggest state (sorry, Alaska, we're talking continental).

2

Early Ukulele Days around the Lone Star State

1917–1963

DOES FORT WORTH EVER CROSS YOUR MIND?

In 1917, you could choose from a variety of ukuleles at the W.C. Stripling Department Store. The "koawood" ukuleles were priced at $4.50 to $9.00 for a high finish and $3.00 and $3.50 for a nice finish. One bonus of buying a ukulele at W.C. Stripling Department Store were the free lessons. The lessons were offered by Mrs. W.C. Butcher on Thursdays.[2]

The W.C. Stripling Department Store was located inside a four-story building in downtown Fort Worth. W.C. Stripling Middle School, named after the department store's founder, was constructed in 1927. Originally built as a high school, it is still in use today as a middle school.

IF YOU EVER GO TO HOUSTON

On March 29, 1917, the M. Paul Jones Orchestra presented "Twilight in Hawaii." The Houston event was a benefit for the Bayland Orphan Home. The event promoters wanted everyone to know that this would not be the usual amateur charity event but a "real" concert. The concert would feature electrical effects, trained players who had put in their rehearsal time and dancers who could really dance. The orchestra featured guitars, mandolins, banjos and ukuleles. Mr. Graham Hall was the lead ukulele player.

START WITH THE NEW UKULELE CLASS THURSDAY
Free Lessons With Every Ukulele We Sell

"Mrs. W. C. Butcher," specialty teacher of stringed instruments, is in charge and will open another free class Thursday. We have ukuleles a plenty at special bargains. Come and take advantage of this offer of free lessons.

Koawood Ukuleles—Beautiful instruments, high finish, at $4.50 to $9.00. Hard wood, nicely finished Ukuleles at $3.50 and $3.00.

Sale third floor.

Q. R. S.
Autograph and Standard Music Rolls

FOR ALL PLAYER PIANOS
June Numbers Ready

Hand played Music Rolls, the now popular word rolls. Come, select the new June numbers; many very catchy numbers; drop in and hear: "Oh, You Daddy," "If You Don't Want Me, Send Me to My Ma," "Kiss Me," "My Hawaii," "Other Eyes," "Tennessee Blues," "'Twas Only An Irishman's Dream," "Wandering Blues." Phone or write us; we will mail you a June Bulletin.

"THE RELIABILITY OF A STORE SHOULD BE YOUR FIRST THOUGHT"

W. C. Stripling

THE PRICE IS THE THING.

A W.C. Stripling ukulele advertisement. *From the* Fort Worth Star Telegram, *May 29, 1917, courtesy of www.newspapers.com.*

W.C. Stripling High School (now a middle school) in the Arlington Heights neighborhood of Fort Worth, Texas. *Photograph from the Jeff Campbell collection.*

Is Anybody Going to San Antone?

Raymond's Hawaiians, playing ukulele and guitar, took the Alamo City by storm in 1922. On August 27, they were the headliner on the *Evening News* radio show. "The band performed a series of dreamy Mid-Pacific songs."[3] Due to their popularity, Raymond's Hawaiians returned to the show on September 3.

Inspired San Antonio radio listeners could take ukulele lessons at the Hawaiian Music School located in the Conroy building.[4]

Out in the West Texas Town of El Paso

Also in 1922, the Associated Press reported that the "banjo-ukulele" was becoming very popular in the border town of El Paso. "The banjo-ukulele, judging from its local use, is almost as popular as the ukulele in this part of the country in 1916, 1917 and 1918, when thousands of high school and college girls were attempting melody on them."[5]

The popularity of the banjo-ukulele was its small size and portability. The four strings made it much easier to play than a traditional five-string banjo. The instrument suited the music of the era, such as ragtime and jazz.

The Stars Are Shining in the East Texas Air

Child Welfare Day was commemorated on February 17, 1926, in Longview, Texas. A musical extravaganza, sponsored by the local PTA, was held at the high school auditorium. The show included readings, singing, a duo featuring a saxophone and clarinet and ukuleles.

The ukulele performances included the girls of the Campus Ward School, the girls of First Christian Church and a song by Mrs. Geo. E. Adams.[6]

Why was the ukulele so popular with women? Jim Tranquada and John King discuss that subject in their book, *The Ukulele: A History*: "Due to the ukulele's portability, young women abandoned the parlor (guitar) and began making music outside as a form of self-expression without parental supervision"[7]

Galveston, Oh Galveston

On May 4, 1926, in Galveston, the Sam Houston Ukulele and Harmonica Club gave their first performance at the city auditorium. Celebrating music week, the club's numbers included "Way Down upon the Swanee River," "The Prisoner's Song," "La Paloma" and "Oh, My Little Augustine."[8]

It's Been a Hard Day's Night

The August 8, 1930 edition of the *Lubbock Morning Avalanche* newspaper advertised that Dexter Curtis, the former "singing bell hop of Amarillo" would be playing for fifty hours at Cammack Drug Company.

Dexter, now calling himself the "ukulele boy," would start at 10:00 p.m. on Thursday and continue until midnight on Saturday. Dexter wanted everyone to know that he couldn't play for fifty hours without the wholesome and delicious food served at Cocanougher's Café.[9]

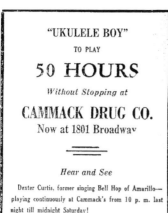

Advertisements for the Ukulele Boy music marathon. *From the* Lubbock Morning Avalanche, *August 8, 1930, courtesy of www.newspapers.com.*

DENTON COUNTY WILL BE RIGHT HERE
WAITING FOR YOU

Over seventy-five North Texas State College students rehearsed for the school's annual water carnival. The carnival was scheduled to be held on May 25, 1950. The student group included swimmers, divers, bathing beauties, square dancers and ukulele players! The music for the carnival was conducted by Floyd Graham and the Aces of Collegeland. Hellen Waller directed the ukulele seven vocal group.

AMARILLO'S WHERE I'LL BE

On February 1, 1951, Amarillo's Paramount Theater hosted the first night of the ukulele contest preliminaries. There would be six straight nights of preliminaries, with two winners selected each night (one in the over-twelve division and one in the under-twelve division). The winners would be selected by the electric applause meter. Also known as a Clap-o-Meter, the applause meter was a device that was used to measure the volume of an audience's applause. The contraptions were very popular on talent shows and television game shows in the 1950s. However, they fell out of favor in the late 1960s. Many times, they were just fraudulent props, with the operator adjusting the device by using their own judgment of the audience's reaction.

Top: Advertisement for the ukulele contest. *From the Amarillo Daily News, January 26, 1951, www.newspapers.com.*

Bottom: Application for the ukulele contest. *From the Amarillo Daily News, February 7, 1951, www.newspapers.com.*

Bobby "Uncle Ukle" Henshaw, who we'll visit in another chapter, was also on hand to entertain with his vaudeville act.

Up for grabs were $2,000 in prizes! The following were the prizes for the over-twelve division:

- Philco refrigerator, with frozen food locker.
- Two-piece luggage set of top-grade rawhide.
- Philco table model combination radio and record player.
- Cadilac electric vacuum cleaner with leatherette storage case.
- $100 U.S. Savings Bond.
- Philco clock radio with an appliance outlet.
- Philco portable radio and automatic toaster.

Then there were the prizes for the under-twelve division:

- Philco cabinet model combination radio with three-speed record changer.
- Philco table model combination radio and record player.
- Deluxe Remington-Rand portable typewriter.
- Monarch boys' or girls' bicycle.
- Fifty-dollar U.S. Savings Bond.
- Philco clock radio with appliance outlet.
- Philco portable radio with battery and electric cord.[10]

This author would like to offer a belated thank-you to Philco for their support of the ukulele community!

At the end of the sixth night of the ukulele marathon, it was time for the grand finale on February 8. Tensions were high at the Paramount Theatre, as the applause meter (or maybe the guy operating the applause meter) rendered its final judgment.

The Kincaid Trio were the winners in the over-twelve competition. The Trio, made up of Clarence Kincaid, Willy Wilson and Callie Moye, drove the audience crazy with their version of "Mule Train." The Trio's presentation was enhanced by the sound effect wizardry of Wilson Moye, a student at Amarillo College.

The multiday contest was produced and conducted by Bobby "Uncle Ukle" Henshaw. The event sponsors were Furr Food Stores, Interstate Theaters and the *Globe News*. A good time was had by all.

I'VE BEEN EVERYWHERE, MAN

On December 13, 1957, Charles R. Ramsden, a scientist, musician and world traveler, gave a presentation in Mexia, Texas. The presentation featured his newly created instrument, the electronic Novatar. The Novatar could reproduce the sounds of trains, animals and other sounds with amazing reality.

> *During his performance, he plays the ukulele in such a manner to as to make it sound similar to a small orchestra. He can make the small instrument sound like a mandolin carrying the melody and at the same time produce the accompaniment and rhythm. Tom-Tom rhythms can be transmitted through the human body to the ukulele because of his new developments in the sub-harmonic field. This produces unheard of effects from the ukulele.*[11]

I'M SENDING YOU A POSTCARD FROM WICHITA FALLS

On March 18, 1961, Mrs. F.D. Burnett hosted the Les Belles Letres Study Club at her home in Wichita Falls, Texas. The theme of the evening's program was "The Birth of Hawaii." Mrs. Thomas shared the history of Hawaii's early years, island politics, becoming a U.S territory, Pearl Harbor and right up to Hawaii statehood in 1959.

The guests wore leis and sang Hawaiian songs accompanied by a ukulele. The hostess served a delectable menu in keeping with the program theme.[12]

I CAN ALMOST SEE HOUSTON FROM HERE

In 1963, The Beatles released their first album, *Please Please Me*, Bob Dylan released *Blowin' in the Wind*, Patsy Cline died in a small plane crash and in Baytown, Texas, the Strugglers Four were born.

Things got rolling when Delores Brister received a guitar for Christmas. An accomplished pianist, Delores had always wanted to learn guitar. Claire Thomas, a neighbor, got her old ukulele out of the closet. Then another Azalea Street neighbor, Teddy Hale, became the arranger. The fourth member, Patricia Southern, played washtub bass.

Full-page story on the Strugglers. *From the* Baytown Sun, *August 22, 1963, www.newspapers.com.*

Other ladies in the neighborhood joined in with ukuleles. Thus, the Strugglers Four became the Strugglers Four and More. The band mainly played backyard parties in the Baytown area. "This is what we do instead of our regular bridge night," one member explained.[13]

3

Homeruns and Ukulele Strums

On March 31, 1916, a group of young Hawaiian men gave a ukulele concert at the University of Texas YMCA.[14] The very next day, these same young men beat the University of Texas Longhorns, 6–4, in a game of baseball.[15] Who were these guys?

The young men were part of a barnstorming baseball team that toured the United States mainland from 1912 to 1916. Promoters—as promoters are wont to do—referred to the team as being from the "Chinese University of Hawaii." In newspapers, this was often shortened to the "Chinese Baseball Team." It's true that the team members were predominately of Chinese ancestry. However, the ballclub also included native Hawaiians and students of other ethnicities.

In fact, there was no such thing as a Chinese University of Hawaii. In Joel S. Franks's well-researched book *The Barnstorming Hawaiian Travelers: A Multiethnic Baseball Team Tours the Mainland, 1912–1916*, he explains that the "Chinese University of Hawaii" was a fabrication, a name created by Hawaiian promoters to sell tickets in America.[16]

The ballclub played exhibitions against semipro teams, Black league teams and college teams. Often, while they were in town, they would serenade the locals with their ukulele-strummed Hawaiian songs.

Many of the American newspaper articles of the day referred to the team members in a derogatory, casually racist manner. These terms are best left in the dust bin of history. But at the same time, these newspapers would praise the players' baseball skills, athletic ability and musical talents.

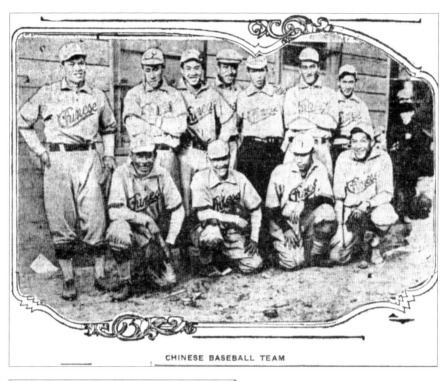

CHINESE BASEBALL TEAM

CHINESE DEFEATED THE LONGHORNS AT AUSTIN YESTERDAY

Times-Herald Special.

Austin, Tex., April 1.—By a score of six to four the Chinese baseball team from the University of Hawaii defeated the University of Texas team this afternoon on Clark field. The game was featured by two home runs, one by each team.

Above: The "Chinese baseball team." The team was really from Hawaii, but they were called "Chinese" by promoters in the United States to sell tickets. *From the* Los Angeles Express, *March 20, 1913, www.newspapers.com.*

Left: The mighty Longhorns defeated! *From the* Waco Times Herald, *April 2, 1916, www.newspapers.com.*

The *Austin American Statesmen* newspaper referred to the team as the "Celestials." The *Celestial Empire* was an old term for China, and in the nineteenth century, the term *Celestials* was used to describe Chinese immigrants in Canada, Australia and the United States.

The star of the Chinese Baseball Team was pitcher Apau "Sam" Kau. Apau was born on September 9, 1890, in Kohala, Hawaii. His parents were

Chinese-born immigrants. Apau's greatest season occurred in 1915, and his best performances were done in Texas.

On March 28, 1915, the Chinese Baseball Team took on the Texas League's San Antonio Bronchos. Although the Bronchos prevailed 3–2, Apau gave up only six hits. The *San Antonio Express* talked with glee about his "wonderful spitter, control and excellent headwork," while stating that his showing was real big-league stuff and that he ranked better than some of the Major League pitchers.[17]

The next month, on April 6, Apau pitched not only a no-hitter against the Baylor Bears but also a perfect game. Apau gave the Bears zero hits and did not walk a batter. Of the twenty-seven Bears at bats, twenty of those were strikeouts. "His spitball was working fine," noted the Travelers' Alfred Yap, "and besides, his other offerings were too puzzling for the Baylor batsmen. All they did was to go up to the batter's box, take the count and slip back to the bench."[18]

The following are some of the other results from the Chinese Baseball Team's 1915 tour of Texas.

MARCH 30: Defeated the Rice University Owls, 3–2.
MARCH 31: Defeated the Rice University Owls, 4–1. (Pitcher George Bo struck out fourteen Owls and gave up only one hit.)
APRIL 2: Defeated the Texas Longhorns, 11–5.
APRIL 3: Lost to the Texas Longhorns, 9–8.
APRIL 4: Lost to the Brenham Brewers, 10–4.
APRIL 5: Defeated the Baylor Bears, 16–8.
APRIL 8: Defeated Austin College (no score reported by the local paper).

In 1916, the ballclub won 37 out of 59 games against college teams and 61 out of 119 against other ballclubs.[19] In addition to the University of Texas game of March 31, the Chinese Baseball Team played quite a few ballclubs in Texas in the spring of 1916. The following are a few of the highlights.

MARCH 29: In Georgetown, Texas, the team earned a hard-fought 3–2 win over an error-prone Southwestern University ballclub.
MARCH 30: In Brownwood, Texas, the team won both ends of a double-header against Howard Payne University. The *Fort Worth Star Telegram* reported that the games were so lopsided, "they were lacking in interest."[20] However, one play aroused controversy, to those paying attention.

A. & M. TO PLAY CHINESE TEAM

Efforts Being Made for Special Car to Carry People Out and Bring Them Back.

Seattle Baseball Club Signs Chinese Player

HONOLULU, Dec. 12.—Vernon Ayau, short stop on the local Chinese baseball team which visits the mainland annually, was signed yesterday to play shor'stop for the Seattle club of the Northwestern league. William Leard, manager of the Seattle club, who is now in Honolulu with a team of touring professionals, offered Ayau the contract. Ayau is said to be the first Chinese baseball player to enter organized ball circles.

CHINESE BASEBALL PLAYER IS KILLED

Apau Kau, one of the best known of the famous Hawaiian-Chinese baseball players who toured this country each year since 1913, was killed while leading his men in one of the recent American drives in France.

Top, left: The *Eagle* newspaper report on an upcoming game between the Fightin' Texas Aggies of Texas A&M and the "Chinese team." *From the* Eagle, *March 29, 1916, newspaers.com.*

Top, right: Vernon Ayau signs a contract to play for the Seattle Indians in the Northwest League. It is believed he was the first player of Chinese descent to sign a professional baseball contract. *From the* Star Tribune, *December 12, 1916, www.newspapers.com.*

Bottom: A newspaper report on the death of Star pitcher Apau "Sam" Kau. *From the* Day, *December 7, 1918, www.newspapers.com.*

With Chin on first base, Ayau dropped a bunt along the first base line. Madden, first baseman, fielded the ball, and while Chin was running to second Ayau stopped and started running back to home plate, along the first base line. Madden, gave chase, and while this little play was going on Chin went to third. Madden finally gave up the chase after Ayau and threw the ball to one of his teammates, to be fielded at first base. This player dropped the throw and Ayau squatted on the first sack. The umpire called first base runner safe.[21]

Should Ayau be out for not running to first base, or did Madden get lured into a bonehead play? The umpire made the correct call, and Madden was left outwitted and embarrassed.

APRIL 2: Fatigue got up with the team from Hawaii. Playing their eighth game in seven days, they were fizzled out by the "Coca-Colas" 25–8. The game was played at Austin's Riverside Park.

APRIL 8: The team took on Meridian College in Meridian, Texas. The men from Hawaii prevailed over their Meridian foes 7–4.

Not every member of the team returned to Hawaii after the 1916 United States tour. Vernon Ayau, the crafty shortstop who embarrassed the Howard Payne University club, signed a contract to play for the Seattle Indians in the Northwest League. It is believed he was the first player of Chinese descent to sign a professional baseball contract.[22]

Star pitcher Apau "Sam" Kau moved to Philadelphia in 2017. He went to work in the sporting goods department of the Lit Brothers Department Store. Of course, he also pitched for the Lit Brothers company baseball team.

During World War I, Apau joined the Pennsylvania National Guard, eventually joining the United Staes Army and then heading to Europe with Company E, 315 U.S. Army Infantry. Only six days before the war ended, on November 5, 1918, Apau was killed on the front lines in Borne-du-Cornouiller, France. Apau was buried in France. However, his remains were eventually returned to Hawaii's Oahu Cemetery. Apau was one of one hundred young Hawaiian men who sacrificed their lives in World War I.

4

The Notorious "Ukulele Jim"

The most infamous politician in the history of Texas politics has to be James Ferguson. If you are familiar with Texas politics, this is quite a race to the bottom. While "serving" as governor, Ferguson was indicted and impeached in 1917. The Texas Senate brought ten charges against Ferguson, which included his political retaliations against the University of Texas, receiving money from unknown sources and the misappropriation of funds. Ferguson served himself instead of the Texas people.

A portion of those funds went to purchase a ukulele. Now, in 1917, a ukulele could be purchased for around $7.50. This seems like something a state governor could afford. However, Ferguson decided to include the ukulele on the governor's mansion expense account. Thus, the disgraced governor became known as "Ukulele Jim."

In 1917, there were no televisions or radio stations and certainly no internet. However, the "Ukulele Jim" moniker went viral across the Lone Star State.

In Tyler, Texas, "Will C. Hogg, representing the Ex-Students Association of the University of Texas, made an appeal to the civic conscious and State pride at a meeting of business men at the Chamber of Commerce this afternoon when he testified, as he termed it, in the case of 'of the people and their university vs. Ukulele Jim and official animosities.'"

The *Georgetown Herald Newspaper* had this to say:

> *But the moral effect of these things accomplished by the henchman of Ukulele Jim and at his dictation, henchmen who could never get the endorsement of the Senate of Texas, renders all the action so tainted with low politics as to be infamous. That our great university should thus become a football and plaything with which a buffoon exhibits his skills at manipulation, is an unspeakable misfortune and a disgrace to Texas.*

The nickname continued to spread across the state into 1918. In the *McKinney Daily Courier-Gazette*, Fitzhugh F. Hill stated, "Wild horses could not tear such a statement from 'Ukulele Jim.' He knows nothing in the world would so completely estrange his dwindling following as the acknowledgement of these charges. He never tells any one he was convicted of using $5,600 State money to pay his own debts."

Texas governor W.P. Hobby relished using the "Ukulele Jim" epithet. "What a good thing for Texas it would have been had 'Ukulele Jim' been possessed of a family cow when he was in the governor's mansion before, for in the time that he was governor the only cow that he milked was the public treasury of the state."

Then on July 20, 1918, Governor W.P. Hobby spoke to a crowd of 2,500 constituents in Crockett, Texas. "And they say down at Austin that 'Ukulele Jim' never did things for nothing.…If 'Ukulele Jim' wishes the Red Cross to receive $1,000, he can bring that about, because I will give $1,000 to the Red Cross if he will tell where he got that suspicious looking money." W.P. Hobby had

Let Us Bring Hawaii to Your Home

"The music of the Hawaiians, the most fascinating in the world, is still in my ears and haunts me sleeping and waking."
MARK TWAIN.

Genuine Hawaiian Ukuleles

Steel Guitars, Tars-patch Fiddles and Kindred Instruments

The Ukulele is the one musical instrument that anybody can play.

Genuine Hand Made of Native Hawaiian Koa Wood from $7.50 Up

Machine Made Instruments for Less

The largest stock of Ukuleles and Hawaiian Instruments in the South.

A complete line of Strings, Pegs, Thimbles, Steels, Cases, Bags and other accessories for all instruments.

We import direct from Honolulu and can sell for less.

An advertisement showing the price of a ukulele in 1917, the price James Ferguson paid for a derisive nickname. *From the* Houston Post, *June 24, 1917, www.newspapers.com.*

served as lieutenant governor while Ferguson was in office and became one of his greatest critics.

Ferguson could not run for governor or any state office after his impeachment, so he did the next best thing: he ran his wife's campaign for governor. Mariam A. Ferguson became the first female governor of Texas, serving two terms (1925–27 and 1933–35).

During her time in office, Mariam Ferguson granted over four thousand pardons. The rumors in Austin were that the pardons were made in exchange for cash payments to "Ukulele Jim." In 1936, Texans voted to pass legislation preventing governors from granting pardons.

And they say Tiny Tim gave ukuleles a bad name!

5
Lee Morse Goes to Texas

Multiple volumes could be written on musicians whose careers were ruined or ended by alcohol addiction. From Hank Williams to Jimi Hendrix, those addictions led to death. Perhaps the most famous example is Brian Jones. Brian Jones was the founder and original leader of the Rolling Stones, even coining the band name. But due to his alcoholism and drug use, he was kicked out of his own band and replaced with Mick Taylor in 1969. Jones spiraled down in his addiction and died of an overdose. For every famous musician, there are dozens whose stories have gone untold. Lee Morse is one of those.

Born Lena Corinne Taylor on November 30, 1897, in Cove, Oregon, Lee was the ninth of twelve children. Her father, John Taylor, was a pastor originally from Texas. Lee was born into a musical family. In fact, before she was born, the family toured Idaho in a covered wagon as the Family Concert Company.

Blessed with a hauntingly deep voice, dissonant with her petite frame, Lee accompanied herself on guitar, ukulele and kazoo. In 1915, she married lumberjack Elmer Morse. By 1918, she was playing shows across the Pacific Northwest. This led to her hitting the West Coast vaudeville circuit and abandoning her husband and young child.

Her recording career began in 1924 when she joined the Pathé label. Her big hits during this time were "Golden Dream Girl" (her own composition), "Ukulele Lady" (which has gone on to be a ukulele standard), "Under the Ukulele Tree," "Telling Eyes," "Daddy's Girl," "An Old-Fashioned

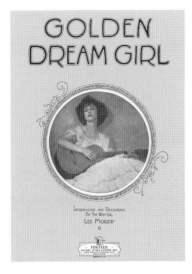 

Left: Sheet music for "Golden Dream Girl." *Public domain.*

Right: Record label for "Under the Ukulele Tree." *Internet Archive.*

Romance," "Blue Waltz," "Deep Wide Ocean Blues" and "A Little Love." Many of these recordings were made under the name "Lee Morse and Her Bluegrass Boys," which had nothing to do with what we now know as bluegrass music. It was during this time that Lee met and supposedly married pianist Bob Downey.[23]

The year 1930 brought an opportunity for Lee Morse to attain superstar status. Lee landed the lead role in Florenz Ziegfield's musical *Simple Simon*, sharing the stage with actor/comedian Ed Wynn. However, during a trial run in Boston, Lee showed up drunk and could not remember her lines. An angered Ziegfield replaced Lee with Ruth Etting. The show was a smashing success and one of its songs, "Ten Cents a Dance," would become a hit record for Ruth Etting.

Later in the year, Lee showcased her deep singing voice and comedy skill in three short films, "Song Service," "A Million Me's" and "The Music Racket." The films were a few rungs below *Simple Simon*.

By 1930, alcohol was Lee's constant companion. Like country superstar George Jones, Lee Morse had stage fright that exacerbated her drinking problem. "I get nervous! I can't stand it! I want to scream!"[24] Due to her stage fright, Lee preferred theater stages to small clubs. However, in the 1930s, clubs dominated the professional music scene, with theater dates hard to find. Her hard drinking would cause her to miss dates and income.

Above, left: An advertisement for a Lee Morse appearance in Fort Worth. *Author's collection*.

Above, right: An advertisement for a Lee Morse appearance in Amarillo, Texas. *From the* Amarillo Globe Times, *December 19, 1938, www.newspapers.com*.

Left: An advertisement for a Lee Morse appearance in Longview, Texas. *From the* Longview News Journal, *December 23, 1935, www.newspapers.com*.

Lee continued to record and appear on radio for the next few years, but she suffered a throat ailment in 1933. Unable to sing, she relocated to Gainesville, Texas, where she stayed with her father's side of the family. Lee attempted to recuperate her voice and rejuvenate her career.

Lee regained her voice and started playing at venues across the Dallas/Fort Worth area. She also made appearances on Texas radio stations. During this time, she lived with Bob Downey in a house on Lake Worth, just west of Fort Worth.

A quick internet search reveals multiple stories that say Lee and Downey owned an "unnamed" club in Texas. To add to the drama, the club burned down in 1939. There was a club between Dallas and Fort Worth named the Sylvan Club that fire destroyed in 1935. Lee had a residency there in 1934 and 1935. The fire destroyed multiple dresses, gowns and bracelets that belonged to her. There is no record that the couple owned the club, but it may be the one that internet jockeys injected in their stories.

Texas did seem to revitalize Lee's music career. With the successful two-year stint in the Dallas/Fort Worth area, Lee began to tour and take engagements across the state. Some of her highlights included performing with Karl Lambertz & His Orchestra in Corsicana, a two week residency at Longview's Carioca Club, a dance at Longview's Petroleum Club and a residency at Amarillo's Paramount Theater. From east to west, Lee definitely saw "Miles and Miles of Texas."

For unknown reasons, Lee and Downey relocated to Rochester, New York, in 1939. It was here that Downey left Lee for a striptease dancer. The severed relationship drove Lee deeper into alcoholism. While in Rochester, she attained only local success, with regional hits and appearances on radio stations. On December 16, 1954, Lee Morse passed away at the age of fifty-seven. It was reported she died from alcohol-related complications.

If you have never heard Lee Morse sing, many of her recordings, both audio and visual, are available online.

6

Bobby "Uke" Henshaw

Ray Canfield, Cliff Edwards, Wendell Hall, Johnny Marvin, Roy Smeck and Bobby Henshaw were some of the big names in the ukulele entertainment world during the 1920s and 1930s.

Bobby Henshaw was not a native Texan; he was born in Wheeling, West Virginia, in 1896. However, he did spend a large portion of his entertainment career in Texas.

Henshaw grew up in a musical family; two of his second cousins would also become famous participants in the music business. Anette Hanshaw was a hugely popular jazz singer on the radio in the 1920s and 1930s. By 1934, Anette had sold over four million records.[25] Henshaw's other cousin was Frank Wayne Hanshaw Jr., who eventually became a talent agent. Some of the celebrities he worked with included Bobby Darin, Jackie Gleason and Nat King Cole.[26]

Bobby Henshaw was a natural when it came to entertaining, singing and playing the ukulele. He was destined to become a vaudeville star.[27] Vaudeville was very popular in the early twentieth century in the United States. Vaudeville featured music, burlesque comedy and dance, often performed by the same artist.

Descriptions of Henshaw's ukulele prowess describe an unearthly talent to make his uke mimic other musical instruments.[28] *Variety* magazine once said Henshaw was "known for his prowess on the ukulele," while the *New York Clipper* entertainment newspaper dubbed him the "Human Ukulele."[29]

A poster for "The Merry Mimic," featuring Bobby Henshaw, at the Majestic Theater in Dallas, Texas, during the week of August 24, 1924. *Photograph courtesy of Mark Miner.*

At the start of the 1920s, Henshaw was playing in Paris, and international stardom was on the horizon. His first wife, Vera Van Atta, was also a performer and became part of his act.[30] In fact, she assisted Henshaw during one of his first Texas appearances. Henshaw performed "The Merry Mimic" at the Majestic Theater in Dallas, Texas during the week of August 24, 1924.[31]

Box Office magazine credited Henshaw with introducing the ukulele to England. He also toured Europe and performed on the BBC.[32] Henshaw also traveled down under, entertaining thousands of Australians.

The growth of cinema would prove to be the downfall of vaudeville, and stars like Bobby Henshaw would have to adjust or become a relic. Henshaw traveled to Hollywood and picked up bit parts in quite a few films. In 1935, he had an unnamed part in the movie *Variety*. In 1949, he appeared in three films. He was a clerk in *Oh, You Beautiful Doll*; had an unnamed part in *Beyond the Forest*, starring Bette Davis; and was a boxing ring announcer in *The Set Up*. Two more film appearance would follow in 1950. Henshaw played an announcer in *Bodyhold* and played Joe the local saloonkeeper in *Return of the Frontiersman*.

Henshaw, always the entrepreneur, also came out with his own signature ukulele. Long before folks could purchase a Gibson Les Paul guitar, there

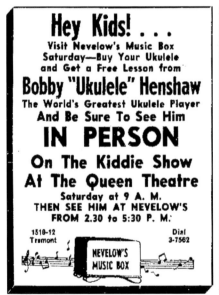 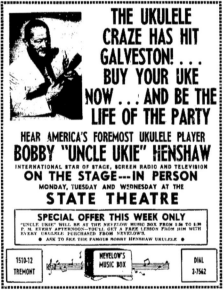

Two advertisements for Bobby Henshaw appearances in Galveston, Texas. *From the Galveston Daily News, July 16 and 22, 1950, www.newspapers.com.*

★ ON THE STAGE ★
● IN PERSON ●

Bobby "UKE" Henshaw

DEAN OF UKULELE PLAYERS
—PRESENTING—
SONGS & NOVELTIES

Accompanied by Gene Smith

● SATURDAY NIGHT ONLY ●
— At 7:00 & 9:00 —

CAMPUS

An advertisement for a Bobby Henshaw appearance in Denton, Texas. *From the* Denton Record Chronicle, *August 18, 1950, www. newspapers.com.*

were Bobby Henshaw baritone ukuleles available to the public. Collectors and luthiers debate whether the Henshaw ukuleles were built by the Vega or Harmony company. The most desirable model was all mahogany and featured a fretboard and bridge made from Brazilian rosewood.[33] Henshaw also had a signature tenor guitar and his own line of baritone ukulele strings.[34]

As the 1950s began, Bobby Henshaw found himself spending a lot of time in the Lone Star State. He made a 1950 appearance at a Houston movie theater, sponsored by the Raymond Pearson Lincoln Mercury auto dealer. The event featured a ukulele contest with a $2,000 grand prize. This was also the era when Henshaw would start using the nickname "Uncle Ukie."

In the summer of 1950, Henshaw had a three-day residency at Galveston's State Theater. In addition to attending the concerts, fans could get a lesson from Uncle Ukie at the local music store as long as they purchased a "Famous Bobby Henshaw Ukulele." While in Galveston, Henshaw also played between showings of current films, such as *Winchester '73*, starring James Stewart and Shelley Winters. Henshaw had a strong following in Galveston. He had played at the old Martini Theater during his vaudeville days. Henshaw had also played Waco's Hippodrome Theater during those times.

In 1953, Mrs. Victor Jones bought the Trinity Theater, which was located in Dallas. Jones appointed Lottie Burt Strong as the theater manager. The refurbished theater needed a jumpstart, and Strong had a flair for showmanship. She brought Henshaw down from Memphis, and he became a regular performer at the Dallas theater.[35]

Henshaw played up his newfound "Texas roots" by starring in the musical *From Broadway to Texas*. Besides Henshaw, the musical also featured Paul Buskirk and the Western String Band.[36] Buskirk was one of the first American musicians to play a solid body electric mandolin.[37]

When Bobby's aunt Kate died in Wheeling in 1954, Bobby was mentioned in her *Wheeling News Register* obituary as residing in Dallas, Texas, at the time.[38]

On February 23, 1955, the *Cisco* (TX) *Daily Press* reported on a performance by Henshaw for the annual Lion's Club Ladies' Night Banquet, held on the previous Monday. The paper referred to him as "Bobby Henshaw of Fort Worth."[39]

By 1960, Bobby Henshaw had moved on to Kansas City. He passed away in Los Angeles in 1969.

The term *rolling stone* is often used in music circles, as a rolling stone doesn't gather moss. Bobby Henshaw rolled his stone around the world multiple times. However, he found a home in Texas, even if it was just for a little while.

This story could not have been told without the help of Mark Miner and his deeply comprehensive genealogy website, www.minerd.com (a sweeping biographical archive of early Pennsylvania German families). Thanks, Mark!

7

The Ukulele-Picking Principal

Lubbock, Texas, has a long tradition of music. The Hub City is the birthplace of Mac Davis, Buddy Holly, Lloyd Maines and his daughter Natalie Maines, Joe Ely, William Clark Green, cowboy songster Andy Hedges and bluesman Delbert McClinton. Texas Tech, Lubbock's major university, jumpstarted the careers of Pat Green, Flatland Cavalry, Wade Bowen and accordionist Ponty Bone. Other Texas Tech alumni include singer-songwriter Bob Livingston and John Denver.

Just outside of Lubbock's city limits is the birthplace of Waylon Jennings, Littlefield, and to the west of Lubbock is the town of Levelland. Levelland is the home of South Plains College, which started the first two-year degree program in bluegrass music and hosts Camp Bluegrass every July.[40]

There are many other talented, unheralded and unknown Lubbock musicians, including Jerry Don Landers. Jerry Don was a track star at Amarillo High School and signed a scholarship with Texas Tech in 1958. Landers studied vocal music at Texas Tech and in 1964, "the singing athlete from Abilene" received his bachelor's degree in music education.[41] Three years later, he completed graduate school with a master's degree in elementary education. His master's thesis was written about using a ukulele in an educational environment.

So, how did the singing athlete from Abilene get involved with the ukulele way out in West Texas?

I first became interested in the ukulele when I heard a friend of mine play it in the car. We had just finished playing volleyball or softball or something

Jerry Don Landers, the ukulele-picking principal. *From the* Lubbock Avalanche Journal, *February 26, 1973, www. newspapers.com.*

like that. Anyway, we got in the car to leave and this fella picked up this ukulele and began playing it. It sounded mellow, full, not like a guitar that often sounds twangy. Anyway, I decided right then that it couldn't be that hard an instrument to play so I went to a local shop and picked one up.[42]

In the early 1970s, Jerry Don's teaching passions were athletics and music. "I knew early on that I wanted to teach music. I also wanted to be a coach because I knew how young boys looked up to their coaches."[43] Jerry Don even talked some of the boys he coached into joining the choir. He started teaching music at Haynes Elementary in Lubbock. The Haynes Ukulele Ensemble grew to have over one hundred members. The ensemble even conducted concerts in places like St. Matthews United Methodist Church.[44]

Jerry Don moved on to become the principal at Lubbock's Dupre and Thompson Elementary Schools. At both schools, he began teaching ukulele in his spare time. He also began a program that taught other Lubbock teachers how to play free of charge. "It doesn't matter if I taught any of these children science or I coached them or taught them music, they always walk up to me and say 'Mr. Landers remember me? You taught me how to play the ukulele.'"[45]

Jerry Don Landers went on to serve as the principal of Spicewood Elementary (Spicewood, Texas) from 1974 until his retirement in 2000.

8

Ukulele Blues

Texas blues guitarists Johnny Winter and T-Bone Walker both started their musical journeys on the ukulele.

I started playing ukulele first for 2 years from age 9 to 11 and got my first guitar and got inspired by blues I heard on the radio that turned me on and I started learning myself.

—*Johnny Winter*[46]

Johnny Winter and his brother Edgar are synonymous with Texas blues. Johnny's first album was the critically acclaimed *The Progressive Blues Experiment*, released in 1968. His younger brother Edgar first found success with the album *Edgar Winter's White Trash*, released in 1971. Over the next five decades, they would tour, record and collaborate, becoming pillars in both the rock and blues communities.

Our dad played the guitar and banjo for fun, and he was also the saxophone player in a swing band when he was younger. When Johnny was 7 and I was 4, my dad showed us our first chords on the ukulele. Johnny and I started playing old blues and folk songs, and we sang gospel music like "Do Lord" and "It Ain't Gonna Rain No More." We liked playing songs by the Everly Brothers and Buddy Holly too. We got good enough to be featured on a local radio program.

—*Edgar Winter*[47]

I didn't want to play guitar because my hands were too small, and those fingering positions were so strange….However, one day Dad said to me "The only two big ukulele guys I can think of are Ukulele Ike and Arthur Godfrey. You're not really made to play ukulele—You ought to try guitar!"

—*Johnny Winter*[48]

Johnny Winter passed away at the age of seventy on July 16, 2014. In 2022, Edgar Winter released a tribute album to his older brother, *Brother Johnny*. The album featured seventeen interpretations of Johnny's best known recordings. Dozens of musicians contributed to pay their respects to Johnny, including Billy Gibbons, Bobby Rush, Derek Trucks, Joe Walsh, John McFee, Keb' Mo', Michael McDonald, Ringo Starr, Waddy Wachtel and Warren Haynes.

I learned all the stringed instruments, like mandolin, violin, guitar, ukulele and banjo.

—*T-Bone Walker*[49]

T-Bone Walker was born on May 28, 1910, in Linden, Texas. T-Bone was born into a musical family. Both of his parents, Movelia Jimerson and Rance Walke, were musicians, and his stepfather, Marco Washington, was a member of the Dallas String Band. Marco was the mentor who taught T-Bone how to play "all the string instruments."

Another influence for T-Bone while he was growing up in Dallas was family friend Blind Lemon Jefferson. As a teenager, T-Bone would "lead" Jefferson around the streets of Dallas, playing for change.

T-Bone Walker eventually headed to Los Angeles, where he became a trailblazer of electric blues, jump blues and West Coast blues. His most famous recording and composition is "Call It Stormy Monday (But Tuesday Is Just as Bad)." The song has become standard and has been covered by hundreds of

Above: Vinyl record label of the T Bone Walker hit, "T Bone Boogie." *Internet Archive.*

Opposite: Instead of blues, soul and R&B, records like T Bone Walker's were referred to as "race records" in the 1940s. *From the* Marshall News Messenger, *April 19, 1946, www. newspapers.com.*

RACE RECORDS

By Johnny Moore

"Traveling Blues"
"Talk of the Town"
"Drifting Blues"
"Groovy"

•

By T. Bone Walker

"T-Bone Boogie"
"Evening"
"Mean Old World Blues"
"You Don't Love Me
 Blues"
"Sail On Boogie"
"I'm Still In Love With
 You"

•

artists, including Prince, James Brown and the Allman Brothers Band. T-Bone Walker passed away in Los Angeles, California, on March 16, 1975, at the age of sixty-four.

Other Texas Bluesmen like Connie Curtis "Pee Wee" Crayton and Major Lee Burke started their musical careers on the ukulele.

Connie Curtis "Pee Wee" Crayton toured with T-Bone Walker in California and had a big hot record with "Texas Hop." He performed at Austin's blues nightclub Antone's only days before he passed away from a heart attack at his home in Los Angeles on June 25, 1985.[50]

Major Lee Brooks was a mainstay of the Austin, Texas blues scene for decades. In 1949, at the age of seven, he started playing ukulele. Then he moved to clarinet, saxophone and then finally piano, the instrument that would become his money maker. Major authored a book, *In the Shadows of Austin*, which chronicled his life as a Black musician in the capital of Texas.[51]

Tip for Ukulele Players

One way to play the blues on your ukulele is to use an open tuning. Tune your first string down from A to G. This takes you from gCEA to gCEG. Strum the strings without fretting, and you'll have a C chord. Barre all four strings at the fifth fret, and you'll have an F chord. Then barre all four strings at the seventh fret and you'll have G chord.

Using a slide, you can play many blues standards, such as "Little Red Rooster," "Ramblin' on My Mind" and "If I Had Possession Over Judgment Day."

9

Tiny Tim's Texas Tour

There is not a more polarizing person in the ukulele community than Tiny Tim, a unique and eccentric performer who managed to stand out from the crowd in the Swingin' Sixties. If you have ever heard his big hit, "Tiptoe Through the Tulips," you'll never forget it.

Some say he set the ukulele back fifty years. Some say he made the ukulele popular again. Others think of him as a novelty act who played a tiny toy instrument and sang in a quivering falsetto voice. If you play ukulele, you're probably going to be compared to Tiny Tim and not Jake Shimabukuro. I share your disappointment.

There are many exceptional biographies about Tiny Tim, including *Eternal Troubadour: The Improbable Life of Tiny Tim*, by Justin Martell and Alanna Wray McDonald, and *Tiny Tim Tiptoe Through a Lifetime*, by Lowell Tarling.[52] So, for our story, I will spare you the long dissertation on Tiny Tim.

However, here's the CliffsNotes version. On April 12, 1932, Herbert Khaury was born in New York City. Young Herbert discovered a love of music and began obsessively listening to seventy-eight records and studying sheet music at the New York Public Library.

He developed a savant-like memory of songs from the 1900s to the 1930s. A self-taught guitarist, Herbert discovered he could sing falsetto (in a high register) and learned ukulele from a method book by Arthur Godfrey.[53]

What followed was a series of talent shows, amateur nights and club gigs. This was the period when his manager dubbed him "Tiny Tim." The 1960s brought Tiny Tim numerous cameos in movies and television, with his big

JULY 1968 / 50¢

discoscene

DISCOSCENE OF SOUTHERN MARYLAND

BIG POSTER INSIDE

Is Tiny Tim for real?

Earth Opera
Joe Tex
Glenn Campbell
Electric Prune
Richie Havens
Blue Cheer
Frank Zappa

Tiny Tim on the cover of July 1968 issue of Discoscene magazine. *Internet Archive.*

break coming on the television show *Rowan and Martin's Laugh In.* In 1968, the album *God Bless Tiny Tim* was released, featuring that unforgettable tune "Tiptoe Through the Tulips."

Tiny Tim was a star! He even appeared on The Beatles' 1968 Christmas record, strumming and singing a version of "Nowhere Man." However, before his Beatles collaboration, Tiny Tim, with his ukulele in a shopping bag, hit the road to cash in on his newfound fame. That road would lead him to the Filmore Auditorium in San Francisco, London's Royal Albert Hall and the Lone Star State.

SAN ANTONIO

Tiny Tim's world tour brought him to San Antonio for a show at the Municipal Auditorium on June 25, 1968. Someone at the *San Antonio Express* newspaper seemed less than enthused about his impending arrival. The paper's anonymous author wrote the following text: "The shaggy giant of American folk falsetto…claims he has been interested in music since childhood.…The shaggy giant's personal habits have been the subject of much attention.…[He's] the shaggy king of the falsetto voice." If you knew nothing about Tiny Tim, by reading this article, you would learn he was "shaggy." The writer did give Tiny Tim a slight compliment at the end of the article: "He is without a doubt the most colorful personality to hit the boards in many a year."[54]

On the Monday before the concert, Sam Kindrick of the *San Antonio Express* was able to interview Tiny Tim. The interview took place in Tiny Tim's room at the Gunter Hotel. Sam's line of questioning totally encompassed the societal divide of the 1960s. The interview started after what Sam described as a "flaccid handshake."[55]

The following excerpts are from the interview that was printed in the *San Antonio Express* newspaper on Tuesday, June 25, 1968.

Sam: Tim, do you like girls?
Tiny Tim: I'm so glad you asked. I simply adore them.
Sam: Okay, Tim, when do you plan to get married?
Tiny Tim: Oh, I couldn't do that. I couldn't get along with one woman for a very long time.
Sam: Tim, you've been accused of affecting an exaggerated air of femininity for shock affect. Like Liberace, some say you are laughing all the way to the bank.
Producing a Bible from his jacket pocket, Tiny Tim stated: Some may think I'm putting them on. Only God and I know the truth for sure.
Sam: Okay, how come you don't wear a mustache and beard like some of the other entertainers?

Tiny Tim Coming To Town Tuesday

Tiny Tim is coming to town!

The shaggy giant of American folk falsetto will appear at the Municipal Auditorium Tuesday, June 25 at 8 p.m.

Appearing with Tiny Tim will be the Yellow Payges a popular California - based rock group.

The concert is billed as a concert — blanket party. Tickets are available at the Municipal Auditorium Box office and are priced at $4.50 and $3.25.

Tiny Tim, who was born Herbert Kaubry, claims he has been interested in music since childhood, when his mother cranked up the Victrola and played "Beautiful Ohio," by Henry Burr.

In a recent article about the shaggy king of the falsetto set, he is quoted as saying the youth of America have catapulted him into the top of the music world.

"The new innocence saved him from obscurity: for the first time in generations, young people began to long for the first time in generations, young people began to long for something pure and sweet and gay," the article says.

He carries his ukelele in an old paper shopping bag, wrapped in a cardigan sweater.

The concert is sponsored by KTSA Radio.

Tiny Tim has appeared on the Rowan And Martin Laugh-In, the Johnny Carson Show, and a number of clubs in New York City, where he was once billed at "Larry Love, The Human Canary."

The shaggy giant's personal habits have been the subject of much attention since his climb to national stardom. He bathes often, using only Packer's Pear Soap, and brushes his teeth with papaya powder, never rinsing his mouth, and has described at length his magic diet of wheat germ, honey, pumpkin and sunflower seeds.

Tiny Tim's new album, "God Bless Tiny Tim," has rocketed into hit charts throughout the country, and though it is difficult to find anyone who really likes the quavering falsetto artist, he is without a doubt the most colorful personality to hit the boards in many a year.

TINY TIM—The shaggy king of the falsetto voice, Tiny Tim, will appear Tuesday at Municipal Auditorium in a concert with the Yellow Pages. Tiny Tim is fresh from New York City and a series of appearances on national television programs.

Howard Duff Daughter Is Creative

HOLLYWOOD — Hollywood interviewers often ask Howard Duff whether he wants his 16 - year - old daughter, Bridget, to pursue a "She has even expressed a desire to write and has come up with a very good idea for a

A story about Tiny Tim. From the San Antonio Express, *June 23, 1968,* www.newspapers.com.

Tiny Tim: How many angels have you seen with mustaches?
Sam: But Jesus had a beard.
Tiny Tim: Only while he was on Earth.
Sam: Do you smoke pot, drink liquor, etc.?
Tiny Tim: Mercy, no, I live on health food and vitamins. My only vice is
that I love the Dodgers too much.[56]

After a few more career-oriented questions, Tiny Tim gave an impromptu hotel room concert. Sam Kindrick was won over, to say the least.

He sang tremulous music that could have flowed from the grave. He came
on with Rudy Vallee stuff, Arthur Fields, Henry Burr and did "If You
Had All of the World and Its Gold" by Stewart Jackson.
Asked if he knew any of the current songs that are popular, the shaggy
(that word again!) *man astonished even his manager as he broke out with*

a Hank Williams yodel that would have the cowboys kicking at the rafters in any hillbilly beer joint.

"You see," Tim grinned, "I am versatile."[57]

In the aftermath of Tiny Tim's Tuesday night concert, some were left dumbfounded. *San Antonio Evening News* columnist Tom Nickell was in that number. In a long, winding, rambling essay titled "What After Tiny Tim?" Tom touched on Elvis, The Beatles, Frank Sinatra, W.B. Yeats, Winston Churchill, William Shakespeare and Francis Thompson.

His column wrapped up with these final words:

Perhaps some as yet undisplayed talent will reveal itself. Or maybe we have come to the point at which an entertainer can be so bad that he or she is considered good. Has the search for distinction on the part of our professional entertainers come to that?

And, if that is—scary as it is—true, where do we go from Tiny Tim? Next on the shelf, ready for the limelight, about to saunter out onto or be carried out and placed on the stage is…God only knows.[58]

DALLAS

Over the next three years, Tiny Tim made three trips to the Big D, Dallas: a record signing on January 23, 1969; a book signing on June 17, 1969; and in September 1970, a nine-day residency at Abe Weinstein's Colony Club.

Tiny Tim's star was still shining bright when he arrived in Dallas for an autograph signing at the Melody Shop record store. One of the store's employees estimated that the event would draw a crowd of about two hundred curious North Texans. Things quickly got out of hand, as the employee's estimate was exceedingly low.

Five thousand teenagers mobbed the record store located in NorthPark Mall. Equipment was damaged, and records disappeared. In the aftermath, news outlets reported the event with words like *pandemonium, swarm, mob scene,* and *human wall.*[59] The Dallas Morning News article included this paragraph.

"Inside, a disheveled Tiny Tim was crouched on the floor behind a row of electric organs.…'Pretend he's not in the store,' directed a manager. Tiny Tim, his shirttail out and his orange, green and brown tie twisted to the side, huddled alone on the floor."[60]

I'm not sure this what Bob Dylan had in mind when he sang "The Times They Are A-Changin'"; however, the times were changing in 1969, when five thousand Texas teenagers could be driven into a frenzy by a falsetto-singing, ukulele-strumming vaudeville performer.

Later in 1969, Tiny Tim published his first book, *Beautiful Thoughts*. The ensuing book tour would bring Tiny Tim to Dallas on June 17. Dallas's WBAT-TV seemed unimpressed by the book.

> *Tiny Tim meets with reporters at the Fairmont Hotel Dallas to talk about a new book called* Beautiful Thoughts. *Tiny is listed as author of the book, which is slightly thicker than a vanilla-wafer and takes about two minutes to read. It includes such advice as "If your name isn't helping you, change it." And it asks the penetrating question "When did you write your mother last?"*[61]

Perhaps the book was a money grab and an opportunity to keep Tiny Tim in the public eye.

The book signing was held at the Sanger-Harris Department Store. Although the store was packed with fans, a second Dallas Tiny Tim riot did not erupt. While he was in town, Tiny Tim took time to meet with the DJs at KLIF Radio.

Tiny Tim returned to Dallas in September 1970 for a residency at the Colony Club. He performed two shows a day for nine days. The Colony Club was owned by Abe Weinstein. The club was located just a few doors down from the notorious Jack Ruby's Carousel Lounge.

The Colony Club was a burlesque joint, a venue not accessible to Tiny Tim's teenage fans. However, by 1970, maybe those teenage fans had moved on to acts like Credence Clearwater Revival or Three Dog Night.

As the world shifted into the 1970s, Tiny Tim's popularity began to diminish. Decades later, he returned to the Lone Star State in an attempt to rekindle his star, a story we'll resume in a later section of this book.

10

In Memory of Mike McAloon

utside of someone like Jake Shimabukuro, there aren't really any ukulele "stars," but across Texas and other parts of the world, there are thousands of ukulele luminaries who teach, inspire and influence others.

Most of these folks never turn a profit through the mighty uke. In fact, for many, it's a money-losing endeavor. Many hours are spent putting together song packets while coordinating and scheduling events.

One of these luminaires was Mike McAloon. Mike was the leader of the Suncreek Strummers ukulele ensemble based in Allen (Collin County), Texas. A Boston native, Mike was also proficient on the guitar, mountain

Mike McAloon (*in the center, dressed in black*) leads the Suncreek Strummers. *Photograph from the Jeff Campbell collection.*

Mike McAloon introduces his band, the Suncreek Strummers. *Photograph from the Jeff Campbell collection.*

dulcimer, mandolin, bodhrán and penny whistle. The Suncreek Strummers not only allowed ukulele players a place to gather, but they also played concerts at churches, senior centers and nursing homes.

I was proud to be a Suncreek Strummer during the years I lived in Collin County. Mike was a knowledgeable, patient teacher (especially the time he had to explain to a well-meaning lady that she could not bring a mandolin to a ukulele jam). Everyone who attended the Sunday afternoon Suncreek Strummer sessions became a better player for their time spent there. It was an environment where you could sense skills and confidence growing all around you.

Michael John McAloon was seventy-five when he passed away at his home in Plano, Texas, on April 1, 2023. Mike is one of the unsung ukulele "stars" of the Lone Star State.

Noel Tardy

A Life Well Lived

musician, teacher, writer, business owner, accountant, massage therapist, IT professional, caterer and nonprofit founder. The saying "more layers than an onion" definitely applied to Noel Tardy.

On August 7, 1950, Noel was born in Dallas, Texas. Noel grew up with a deep-seated love of music, singing in choruses and playing in bands and orchestras. After high school, she enrolled at Texas Woman's University (TWU) as a music major.

Noel studied classical guitar and also played bass and guitar with the Texas Woman's University Serenaders. These efforts led to a stage band scholarship at TWU. While at TWU, Noel was a member of the Aglaians Literary-Social Club, the Resounding Harmony mixed chorus and the Women's Chorus of Dallas.

After college, Noel pursued many professions that included IT, message therapy and accounting. She also honored her Czech heritage, opening Two Hot Czechs, a catering company, with her mother.

Noel later attended the University of Hawaii, and then in 2000, a few strums on a ukulele sent her life and musical compass in a new direction. Returning to Dallas, Noel found it difficult to find ukulele strings, accessories, tablature and instruction books and sheet music.

"There really wasn't even much available on the Internet at the time," *she says. So she became the Ukulele Lady of Dallas, selling instruments* *and other uke-related stuff online at ukeladymusic.com.* [In 2004], *she*

opened a ukulele shop in East Dallas, and she's already finding ways to give back to the community. The store is inside Keep U N Stitches, the custom embroidery shop that fellow ukulele enthusiast Gina Volpe opened at Buckner and Northcliff in 1997. The shop, which Tardy thinks could be the only uke shop in Texas, also sells handmade guitars, amplifiers, music books, CDs and anything ukulele related. "You can play so many genres of music on a ukulele," Tardy says. "It's little and it's portable. You can take it anywhere." She and Volpe started a nonprofit, Ukes in the Classroom Texas, to help provide music study in North Texas elementary schools. So far, they've given 24 ukuleles to two schools, and they provide free instruction for the music teachers. "Ukulele is an ideal instrument to introduce kids to music," Tardy says.[62]

Noel and Gina met at one of the Dallas Ukulele Headquarters events led by Mark Levine. With Mark's assistance, Noel produced the Lone Star Ukulele Fest. The festival was held from 2009 to 2013.

The Lone Star Ukulele Fest brought in many talented ukulele musicians from around the world. James Hill, Gerald Ross, The Barnkickers, Kimo Hussey, Debbie Porter and Pops Bayless are just a few of the accomplished Ukesters who appeared at the Fest.

It was during this time that Noel was diagnosed with cancer. Much of her energy was expended going through associated challenging treatments. In 2012, she cofounded the musical duo Spirit Runners Music with fellow cancer survivor Kate McLennan. The duo performed not only in Dallas but also in Madrid and the Czech Republic.

On the duo's GoFundMe page, Noel explained, "Our music partnership developed due to both of us being cancer survivors. Our mutual love of

Noel Tardy. *Photograph courtesy of Tom Steele.*

music as a healing modality, and our passion for ukulele music forged a friendship and a richly diverse musical sound. We birthed Spirit Runners Music as a resource for people facing health challenges and their loved ones."[63]

In 2013, Noel and Kate released the album *Choose Love.* Noel and Kate trade vocals on the CD, which includes a mix of covers and originals written by Kate. The

Noel Tardy (*left*) performs at the 2009 Lone Star Uke Fest. *Photograph courtesy of Dallas Ukulele Headquarters.*

instrumentation is predominantly tenor ukulele, along with a bass uke, an eight-string ukulele, a soprano ukulele and a baritone ukulele. The album is a musical message of hope in trying times.

Noel possessed literary skills in addition to her musical talent. She wrote the children's book, *KoKo Takes a Road Trip*, along with multiple essays and articles. Noel was a 2017 Words of Women recipient for an essay about her grandmother.

Unfortunately, Noel Tardy passed away on November 7, 2017. She influenced and lifted up more people than most of us will meet in our lifetimes. That's truly a life well lived.

> *Bob and I met Noel in 2004 through our daughter Ann when she and Noel were singing with The Women's Chorus of Dallas. You could say that Noel kick-started my ukulele playing because prior to that I was just singing along with Bob when he played guitar or ukulele. I started out playing the soprano uke, learning as I went, and playing with Noel's group, known at that time as UFO. We played at luaus, charity events, and just for fun. I*

have since moved on to playing the baritone uke, but I can honestly say that I probably would not be playing ukulele if I had not met Noel. She has touched many lives with her love of music.[64]

—Judy Sparkman (Judy and her Husband Bob lead the North Dallas Baritone Ukulele Group, also known as BUGS.)

Spirit Runners Choose Love, Feat. Kate McLennan & Noel Tardy *is available digitally at Amazon.com, as is the children's book* KoKo Takes a Road Trip.

12

Ebby Halliday

Do something for someone every day.
—Ebby Halliday

If you have driven around Dallas, Texas, I bet you've seen an Ebby Halliday "For Sale" sign in somebody's front yard. Ebby Halliday (1911–2015) was known as the "First Lady of Real Estate." Ebby was also a philanthropist, singer and a ukulele player.

In the 1940s, she succeeded in a male-dominated business, real estate. Ebby Halliday built one of the largest independent real estate companies from a one-woman business, quite an accomplishment considering that women could not even have their own checking account until 1974, when the Equal Credit Opportunity Act (ECOA) was passed. So, how does a girl born in Arkansas become one of the most successful businesspersons in the state of Texas?

Ebby was born on March 9, 1911, in Leslie, Arkansas. Her birth name was Vera Lucille Koch. Unfortunately, Vera lost her father at a young age. The family relocated to Kansas to live with her grandfather. On Saturdays and during the summer months, Vera worked at the J.B. Case department store. Vera graduated from high school in 1929.

This was during the Great Depression, so college was an impossible dream. Vera moved to Kansas City for new opportunities. She went to work for the Consolidated Millinery as a hat salesperson.

Vera's can-do attitude earned her a promotion to the Jones Department Store in Omaha, Nebraska. There, she became the manager of the Hat Box.

Ebby and her ukulele. *Image courtesy of Ebby Halliday papers, DeGolyer Library, Southern Methodist University, DeGolyer Library, Southern Methodist University.*

By 1938, Vera was in Dallas, working for W.A. Green Store. In 1945, Vera married Claude William "Holly" Halliday in New York State. That same year, she adopted the name "Ebby." Eventually, Ebby leased a space in an old house and opened Ebby's Hats.

One of Ebby's clients was married to Clint Murchison Sr. (the father of Dallas Cowboys founding owner Clint Murchison Jr). Murchinson was failing miserably at trying to sell some new houses. Murchinson issued Ebby a challenge: "If you can sell my wife these crazy hats, maybe you could sell my crazy houses." It was 1945, and very few women were in real estate, but Halliday felt excited and passionate about the prospect. She sold her hat business to her designer and quickly set about selling all fifty-two houses in the development. Halliday went on to build the largest independently owned residential real estate firm in Texas and one of the largest in the United States.[65]

The following are some of the honors Ebby acquired over the years.

- Outstanding Woman in Real Estate in the Southwest (1956)
- Texas Realtor's Realtor of the Year (1963)

- Distinguished Service Award from the National Association of Realtors
- Medal of Honor for Distinguished Service from the International Real Estate Federation (1985)
- Dallas's Linz Award (2008)

Halliday lived by her motto "do something for someone every day." She became as famous for philanthropy as she was for her real estate prowess. The following are a few of the organizations Ebby supported.

- The first woman president of the North Dallas Chamber of Commerce.
- President of the Greater Dallas Planning Council.
- President of Keep Texas Beautiful.
- Vice-president of the Beautify Greater Dallas Association.
- Director of the Texas United Fund.
- President of the Thanksgiving Square Foundation.
- She was a board member of the St. Paul Medical Foundation.
- She was board chair of the Communities Foundation of Texas.
- She was a national trustee of the Foundation Fighting Blindness.
- She opened the Ebby House and Ebby's Place, both to help disadvantaged women.

Ebby was also well known for her singing and ukulele playing. Whether she was at a business function or meeting with newly employed real estate agents, Ebby would use the ukulele to enhance her humor and charm. "You know I really can't play the ukulele or sing, but it helps to have a shtick, everybody needs a shtick."[66] Ebby always brought her ukulele when she attended meetings and other civic and business events.

In 2002, the southwest region of the American Jewish Congress honored Halliday with its prestigious "Flame of Honor" award. Ben Tinsley, the CEO of the Southwest Jewish Congress, remembers that night well: "Ebby not only accepted her award with eloquent charm and humor, but she also entertained the audience with her ukulele."[67]

At Ross Perot's one hundredth birthday party, Ebby sang a song she wrote for Perot while strumming her ukulele. Part of Ebby's "shtick" was taking well-known songs and rewriting the lyrics. So, "Happy days are here again / The skies above are clear again / So let's sing a song of cheer again" became "Happy days are here again / Interest rates are down again / Fannie Mae

The Dallas Ukulele Headquarters perform for Ebby Halliday in 2013. *Photograph courtesy of Dallas Ukulele Headquarters.*

is buying loans again." The Coke commercial song "I'd Like to Teach the World to Sing" was also rewritten. "It's the Real Thing" became "It's the Relo Thing."

The popular 1920s song "Five Foot Two, Eyes of Blue (Has Anybody Seen My Girl?)" also got the Ebby rewrite. The original lyrics are "Five foot two, eyes of blue / But oh, what those five foot could do / Has anybody seen my girl? / Turned up nose, turned down hose / Never had no other beaus. / Has anybody seen my girl?" Ebby turned it into an ode to the wonders of Irving, Texas: "Just northwest…of Big D / There's a town you need to see / Irving is the place to be / Friendly folks…you get to know / Believe it when they tell you so / Irving is the town for me."

For decades, Ebby had a relationship with the Plano Symphony Orchestra. Orchestra director Hector Guzman recalled "[Ebby] breaking out her ukulele on more than one occasion at the Symphony's 1990s-era concert galas." "She shocked everyone," he said with a laugh.[68] May all ukulele players be so bold.

Ebby also had a great relationship with local ukulele community. At Ebby's one hundredth birthday party, members of the Dallas Ukulele

Headquarters were the openers for birthday party headliner, Tony Orlando. Then on June 4, 2013, the Dallas Ukulele Headquarters Community Ukulele Band played in honor of Ebby at the Entrepreneurs for North Texas, Spirit of Entrepreneurship Event in Dallas.

On September 8, 2015, Ebby Halliday passed away from natural causes. She was 104 years old. Halliday not only broke new ground for women in real estate and philanthropy, but she also created a cheerful legacy through her music and wit. Those who got to see her play her ukulele and sing her amusing rewrites of popular songs will cherish those memories.

13

Peter Rowan

Honorary Texan,
Ukulele-Strumming Bluegrass Boy

P eter Rowan could be considered the Jackie Robinson of bluegrass music. For those who do not follow baseball (my wife tells me these people do exist), Jackie Robinson was the first African American to break into the Major Leagues in 1947. Peter Rowan didn't cross the color line, but he did cross the Mason Dixon line.

In the early 1960s, it was believed the northerners (Yankees) could not perform bluegrass music. Sure, Bill Keith from Boston had joined Bill Monroe's Bluegrass Boys in 1963, but he was strictly an instrumentalist. The attitude remained that there was no way a Yankee could sing bluegrass. Boy did Massachusetts-born Peter Rowan prove them wrong.

Rowan was born on July 4, 1942, in Wayland, Massachusetts. When Peter was four years old, his uncle Jimmy returned from his navy service in Hawaii. Uncle Jimmy came bearing Hawaiian treasures: grass skirts, coconut bras and a Martin ukulele he won in a card game. Uncle Jimmy must have been quite the character. Peter said his first musical experience was hearing Uncle Jimmy playing the Hawaiian classic "My Little Grass Shack in Kealakekua, Hawaii." "He was my hero, and he taught me chords to 'Five Foot Two,' 'Aint She Sweet,' 'Bye Bye Blackbird.'...So, I learned those songs first."[69] Peter's uncle also taught him how to play guitar.

Rowan's teenage years were spent square dancing, visiting Boston's legendary country music club the Hillbilly Ranch and forming his first band, the three–electric guitar outfit called The Cupids. In the 1960s,

Rowan switched to the acoustic guitar, influenced by the blues and folk revival. He also started listening to the Country Gentlemen and The Stanley Brothers.

Fellow Bay Stater Bill Keith became part of Rowan's big breakthrough as an artist. "Bill Keith had been a 'Bluegrass Boy,' and he hired me to play some dates with Bill Monroe in New England....Bill suggested I come to Nashville, "I can help you!" I had been playing with Joe Val in [the] Boston area. Everyone said I should go for it...and I did."[70] In 1964, Rowan became part of the greatest band in bluegrass history, Bill Monroe and his Bluegrass Boys, and how that Yankee boy could sing.

Monroe felt that Rowan sounded a lot like himself. "When the two harmonized together, they were said to reach 'heavenly heights.'"[71] Rowan and Monroe also cowrote a song that would become a bluegrass standard, "Walls of Time." However, by 1967, Rowan had left the Bluegrass Boys. Perhaps Monroe's style was bit confining to young man in the '60s with wanderlust and an explorer's heart.

After leaving Bill Monroe's band, Rowan's musical journey took him down one thousand roads. He first formed the Bluegrass Dropouts with David Grisman, then the Earth Opera and then Sea Train (1969–72) with Richard Greene and drummer Roy Blumenfeld.

It was with Sea Train that Rowan grew weary of the life of a touring musician. With only a few dates left on their tour, Rowan decided to leave the band. The last shows for Rowan took place in Houston and San Antonio, and the last show was in Washington, D.C., a week later.

The morning after the Houston show, Rowan took a walk through the neighborhood. He was struck by two things: the mix of Latinos and white people and the contrast of his then-current lifestyle. After the San Antonio show, he told the band he was staying for the week and would meet them in Washington, D.C., for his last concert with the band.

"The morning after the Houston show, I walked around and noticed people on their porch, friendly, white and Hispanic. It was so down-home and a contrast with the rock-and-roll lifestyle."[72] The Houston experience led to his decision to spend a week in Old San Antone.

> *I spent my time wandering the streets. You could hear Conjunto music and community choirs. There was a taqueria that sold tacos, two for $1.25, but you had to go next door to the pool hall to buy a beer. I was struck by the simplicity compared to the grind of the music business, set lists and traveling.*

I wandered to the westside and its wooden buildings. I heard a trumpet coming from one. There, on a rickety stage, were three musicians: accordion, trumpet and snare drum. Not bluegrass but similar to bluegrass in using the instruments at hand. I was the only "gringo" there. It was my first experience with another culture.

After Rowan spent a week in San Antonio, his musical path eventually led him to Nashville. However, the call of the Lone Star State would eventually lead him back down south.

Texas singer-songwriter Robert Earl Keen moved to Nashville in 1986. Rowan explained how their friendship developed: "Robert lived just down the street from me, and we had a mutual friend in Ken Levitan (manger for Lyle Lovett, Nanci Griffith and New Grass Revival). We became soulmates and even wrote together. Robert had a regular gig at the Station Inn but couldn't find footing here and went back to Texas."[73]

Also, Rowan met Hank Harrison, the bandleader for the San Antonio–based group Tennessee Valley Authority. Through jamming and developing a friendship with the TVA, Rowan met Flaco Jimenez, the Texas accordion king. Rowan and Jimenez gigged around Austin. They also recorded two albums together: *San Antonio Sound* in 1983 and *Live Rockin' Tex-Mex* in 1984.

In 1990, Rowan made the move to Texas, purchasing what he described as a "two-room shack in Blanco." He continued, "Texas was an escape from the mundane of Nashville. A place to grow personally. You could hear the sound of cattle, and every Tuesday morning, there was a livestock auction that started at 5:30 a.m. There were neighbors talking over the fence."[74]

In Texas, Rowan had the chance to rekindle friendships with musicians like Junior Brown and Robert Earl Keen. Junior Brown is famous for his guit-steel, a combination guitar and steel guitar. Rowan was there when Brown debuted the instrument in Nashville in 1985.

Cover from the album *The Peter Rowan & Tony Rice Quartet*. Bluegrass guitarist Tony Rice is just one of many artists Peter Rowan has collaborated with over the years. That list includes folks like Jerry Garcia of the Grateful Dead and, of course, the many talented musicians of Hawaii. *Photograph courtesy of Peter Rowan.*

Rowan formed the Texas Trio with Bryn Davies Bright (bass) and Billy Bright (mandolin, Two High String Band/Wood & Wire) in 1999 after sharing the stage at the Old Settlers Music Festival. The band toured across the country and with the Tony Rice. This eventually led to two albums: *You Were There for Me* in 2004 and *Quartet* in 2007. Sharon Gilchrist played mandolin on the *Quartet* album after the divorce of Bryn and Billy.

Another project in this period was *High Lonesome Cowboy*. The *High Lonesome Cowboy* album featured Rowan along with cowboy songster Don Edwards and the guitar virtuosos Tony Rice and Norman Blake. The album won best traditional folk album at the forty-fifth Grammy Awards.

In 2012, the Texas-based Bluegrass Heritage Foundation awarded Rowan its Bluegrass Star Award. The award was given at the annual Bloomin' Bluegrass Festival in Farmers Branch, Texas.

However, by 2017, the Texas Hill Country was changing, and Rowan made the move to Marin County, California. In an interview with the *Marin Independent Journal*, Rowan stated: "'You know, there's a great charm to the Texas hill country,' he says. 'I went there for the less-hectic lifestyle than Nashville was offering at the time. And when you're there, you think it's the place to be. But it's gotten so crowded. The hills are limestone, so they keep putting in grapevines and wineries. People think it's the South of France.'"

The year 2017 also saw Rowan go back to the beginning, revisiting Uncle Jimmy and his Martin ukulele. Rowan recorded the album *My Aloha* in Honolulu. The eleven songs on the album sound like traditional Hawaiian tunes. However, they are all originals, written by Peter Rowan.

One of the songs, "Jerry in the Deep Blue Sea," is a tribute to the Grateful Dead's Jerry Garcia. Rowan played with Garcia, David Grisman (mandolin) and Vassar Clements (fiddle) in the bluegrass band Old and in the Way in 1973 and 1974. Fittingly, one of the songs on the album is titled "Uncle Jimmy": "Uncle Jimmy, Uncle Jimmy, Uncle Jimmy in the navy. / He charmed the hula girls with ukulele."

Rowan called in his Hawaiian friends to back him on the project. The *My Aloha* band included Uncle Mike Souza on electric bass, Douglas Po'oloa Tolentino on harmony vocals and ukulele, Jeff Au Hoy on slide guitar and upright bass and Kilin Reece on guitar and mandolin.

Rowan talked about how the ukulele led him to create an album of Hawaiian music:

> *Well, that's the first instrument I learned, the ukulele. It had never dawned on me that it was going to open any doors. A few years ago, a friend of mine*

made a baritone uke, a nice one, so I started playing it, and songs started coming. When I would go over there [to Hawaii], you know, I'd hit the water and swim and then come back to the instruments and play. You're in a zone. It's a different zone. And the songs started coming. It's more of a watery thing, a little bit sunbaked. That's really why I did the project, because I was writing the songs.[75]

Rowan still maintains his Texas ties. Max Bacca called Rowan in 2018 and suggested some Texas shows with his own Tex-Mex conjunto band, Los TexManiacs; Peter reunited with Flaco for the Texas shows. "It was like old times," said Rowan. "Los TexManiacs are a modern progressive bunch of guys who grew up musically listening to what I played with Flaco. They know my songs, and they include me as part of their tradition!"[76] The Rowan-Bacca project goes by the name Free Mexican Airforce, named after one of Rowan's songs.

From Boston to Nashville, Texas, California and Hawaii, what road will Peter Rowan pursue next?

Austin's Dos Maestros

The Austin Ukulele Society is the cornerstone of the Bat City ukulele community.[77] Austin is also the home of two of the top ukulele instructors in the United States, Pops Bayless and Kevin Carrol. They are not only outstanding musicians and entertainers but also in-demand instructors across the country.

KEVIN CARROLL

Kevin Carroll is a great entertainer and educator. He's come up to do workshops for us, and they were always well thought out and fun. Very generous with his time.
　　　　　　　—Mark Levine (founder of Dallas Ukulele Headquarters)

There are hundreds of stories about aspiring musicians heading to Austin, Texas, dreaming of the "Live Music Capitol of the World," a place to pursue their dreams and aspirations. Kevin Carroll's story is one of those tales. Kevin left his native home of Boise, Idaho, for Austin in 1991.

During his time in Austin, Carroll toured Japan as a solo artist, signed a recording deal with an Italian record company, played guitar for the Flatlanders & Charlie Robison and appeared at Austin City Limits. From the outside, it looked like Carroll was living the dream. However, financial difficulties and other afflictions were taking their toll.

By 2011, the roots-rocking guitarist was having problems with his shoulder, which would dislocate while on stage. The aftermath of an old basketball injury was giving him excruciating pain and discomfort. A local physical therapist offered him treatment in exchange for teaching the therapist's daughter how to play the ukulele. "I had never played one," Carroll, said. "Never even picked up one....Like so many people, I thought they sounded terrible," he said. "But I had never heard actual music played on one. That makes me a great advocate for the instrument now. I know what it's like to think: 'Really? You're going to play music on that thing?'"[78]

Within a year of his physical therapist's offer, Carroll had mastered the ukulele, a feat that is probably not that difficult for a professional guitarist. After all, if you capo your guitar on the fifth fret and play only the first four strings, you've got a ukulele!

Fast-forward to 2024, and Kevin Carroll is one the most popular, in-demand ukulele instructors in North America. Carroll has taught at the Hawai'i Island Ukulele Retreat, the Royal City Ukulele Festival (Canada), the Strathmore UkeFest, the West Coast Ukulele Retreat, Gaithersburg UkeFest, Oregon's Ukulele Band Camp and many others. Carroll has been certified as a level 3 teacher in the James Hill Ukulele Initiative and as an elementary educator in the state of Texas.

Kevin Carroll excels in taking the instrument beyond Hawaiian songs and the popular/standard covers. Carroll has done this through programs he has created, such as Ukestra, the Art of the Ensemble Series, Ukulele Jazz Club, the Ukulele Blues Club and Ukulele Ceilidh.

Ukestra, based in Austin, is a structured ukulele orchestra. It gives ukulele players the opportunity to play in a structured ensemble. Music is written for standard re-entrant ukuleles, ukuleles with a low G string and Ubass. Carroll also offers a three book series titled Art of the Ensemble. The books provide guidance for ukulele groups to transform themselves into an orchestra.

Ukulele Jazz Club and the Ukulele Blues Club are both yearlong courses offered on Zoom. Both courses go deep into each genre exploring jazz and blues improvisation, blues finger picking and turn arounds, theory and chord studies. The two courses also delve into the classic standards in each genre.

Ukulele Ceilidh is a course in Irish-Celtic reels, polkas, a hornpipe and jigs. The book contains eighteen traditional tunes transposed into tablature for ukuleles. During the COVID-19 pandemic, Carroll taught an online workshop on the Ukulele Ceilidh material. In a review for her blog, *Concert Blog*, pianist (and ukulele enthusiast) Anne Ku praised the book.

Kevin Carroll teaches a workshop in Carrollton, Texas. *Photograph courtesy of Dallas Ukulele Headquarters.*

Author Kevin Carroll makes no assumptions. He not only defines the words in the title but also how to pronounce them. It's obvious that considerable research went into producing this book, to get the eighteen traditional Celtic tunes into standard notation and ukulele tablature with chord diagrams.

I consider music for ukulele the ultimate test in simplicity. Just how easy can you make it for someone to sight read with others? Song sheets have achieved that goal for songs the singers are already familiar with. What about instrumental music that is unfamiliar? Carroll introduces the world of ceilidh tunes for the ukulele player by describing and annotating strumming and picking patterns.[79]

In addition to these programs, Carroll gives private lessons and teaches edUKEcation workshops (a curated collection of ukulele arrangements); "Fab Four Strings," which offers ukulele players a Beatles ukulele workshop; and an African Ukulele Workshop Series.

Kevin Carroll also produces Ukulele Joy!, a semiannual showcase for Carroll's ukulele students. It's an opportunity for them to show off their newfound skills in public. The shows are currently held at Kick-Butt Café. Admission is free, and the shows are open to players of all ages. The nineteenth Ukulele Joy! was held on April 21, 2024.

Besides the many ukulele books Carroll published, in 2014, he released the album *resolUKEtion*. Not just another ukulele album, *resolUKEtion* is a bundle of original tunes, with slide playing, Texas blues, jazz, folk, funk and a hint of George Harrison/Ravi Shankar. Carroll's mentor, James Hill, had high praise for the album. "I've been playing the ukulele for 25 years, and I thought I'd heard it all. Then Kevin comes along with this *ResolUKEtion* album and brings a fresh perspective to the instrument. His love for folk, blues and roots music really comes out. Plus, he's a really nice guy and a passionate teacher of the instrument."[80]

Kevin Carroll arrived in Austin as a hotshot guitar player. He is now a ukulele virtuoso, teacher and creator, spreading "ukulele joy." Our dreams may not turn out as expected, but sometimes, they flourish into something better than we could have imagined.

POPS BAYLESS

He's always tried to have this bad-ass persona, but he's really this incredibly talented, sweet guy.
—Mark Levine (founder of Dallas Ukulele Headquarters)[81]

With his shaved head, goatee and handlebar mustache, Austin's Pops Bayless looks more like a boxing coach than a ukulele teacher. For over twenty years, Pops has been one of the most in-demand ukulele instructors across the United States.

In addition to conducting numerous workshops, he has taught at Kansas City's Folk Alliance International, the Midwest Ukulele Festival, the San Antonio Ukulele Festival, the Augusta Heritage Center, Blue Stone Folk School, the Ukulele Expo, Hill Country Acoustic Music Camp and the Lone Star Uke Fest.

Pops is known for being generous and amazingly patient with his students, whether they're budding professionals or folks just getting started. Mark Levine said about Pops,

He would come down to San Antonio in the years that they were holding the Ukulele Festival. He would circulate and interact with everyone there, as well as providing an amazing performance. His teaching skills are extraordinary. One of my favorite explanations had to do with fingernails. He was talking about how long fingernails were useful for fingerpicking on a uke. His explanation was long and entertaining, and involved suggesting that cutting your fingernails straight instead on a curve gave them much more strength.

He would drive up to Dallas often in the early days of Dallas Ukulele Headquarters to share music and some teaching with us. Back then, I didn't even know it was appropriate to offer money as a thank you. He actually never drove, but always got a friend to do the driving. Very generous with his time and energy. We also came down to Austin several times for workshops with him.[82]

—Mark Levine

So, how did the man who has helped so many on their ukulele journey get started on the four-stringed instrument? Pops explains, "I got into the ukulele when I was in a string band called the Asylum Street Spankers. We played a lot of old school tunes, some of them Hapa Haole. So we used ukes on some tunes and when I left them in 1999 I decided the uke was my next thing."[83]

The Asylum Street Spankers were an Austin-based acoustic roots band that started in 1994. The band was known for covering early jazz standards and performing their own risqué, tongue-in-cheek tunes. Pops was a member of the band for five years (1994–99). His role in the band was that of a songwriter, multi-instrumentalist and frontman.

After leaving the Spankers, Pops started a new band, Shorty Long. Shorty Long was a ukulele-driven band that recorded three albums over their ten-year existence. Pops managed the band and booked their shows. Austin Ukulele Society founder, Bob Guz, was a member of Shorty Long.

As an accomplished songwriter, Pops feels the ukulele is one of the best instruments for composition. Let's just say that some of his songs are a bit off color. Mark Levine talks about learning Pop's songs in a unique environment, "One time, the location we found to do it was in a church, and I always thought it was interesting learning some of his bawdy songs in a church. Fortunately, lightning never struck us."[84]

One of his songs, "Flamin' Ukulele in the Sky," has become a ukulele jam standard. (Lyrics published with the permission of Pops.)

Left: Poster for a Pops Bayless workshop. *Photograph courtesy of Dallas Ukulele Headquarters.*

Below: Pops Bayless performing at the Bath House Cultural Center in Dallas, Texas. *Photograph courtesy of Dallas Ukulele Headquarters.*

I was a banker, cash was my need,
I worshiped mammon, I bathed in greed
And then a vision, flashed 'fore my eye-eye-eyes,
of a flamin' uku-le-le in the sky

Chorus
That flamin' ukulele in the sky, lord, lord.
That flamin' ukulele in the sky
It had four sweet golden strings,
and the sound of angel wings
That flamin' uku-le-le in the sky.

I was a preacher; I fell from grace.
Got caught nekkid, at Mabel's place
I asked forgiveness, and God's re-ply-y-y,
was a flamin' uku-le-le in the sky

Repeat Chorus
I was a lawyer, had all the luck,
I bent the truth, just to make a buck
But now it's my turn, to testi-fy-y-y,
'bout a flamin' uku-le-le in the sky

Repeat Chorus
So as you wander, life's rocky road,
and start to stumble, beneath the load
Your sweat and toil, will sancti-fy-y-y,
that flamin' uku-le-le in the sky

Repeat Chorus
Slowly
It had four sweet golden strings,
and the sound of angel wings
That flamin' uku-le-le in the sky-------y!

Pop's original music has been used in the film *No Vacancy* and in the MTV television show *Austin Stories*. In 2006, his Off-Broadway musical, *American Novelty*, premiered at the Theater for the New City in New York.

As of 2024, Pops is still writing and composing. "As for a new album, I don't know. I might not record the new stuff. It's not cost effective, what with the outlets paying me two cents per play. I'm tired of getting ripped off by billionaires. I might just go to a format where the only way to hear me is live."[85]

If you have the chance to meet Pops Bayless, don't be intimidated by his outward persona. You'll miss the chance to learn from one of the best in the business. Mark Levine said, "There is a gruff quality to him.…The truth is, he's a wonderful guy."[86]

15

Cas Haley

Reggae music is very popular in the United States. Some of the American cities known for reggae are New York, Chicago, Miami, Los Angeles, Honolulu and Paris, Texas. Paris, Texas? Yes, Paris, Texas, is the home of reggae artist and ukulele player Cas Haley.

So, how does a young man from rural East Texas get involved in reggae music? Cas laughingly explained, "It kind of came to me from a couple different angles. My parents were both musicians and had a very eclectic musical palette. So I grew up in a house were world music and reggae was heard from time to time…the second angle was through skateboard culture of the '90s."[87]

Haley's unique blend of reggae and folk music thrust him into the national spotlight in 2007. He auditioned for and ended up finishing in second place on the second season of *America's Got Talent*. One of the judges, Piers Morgan, said his audition performance, a cover of "Walking on the Moon," was better than Sting's original version.

The second-place finish guaranteed Haley a record deal with the producers of *America's Got Talent*. However, in the tradition of Texans Willie Nelson and Waylon Jennings, Haley's Texas independence streak would not allow his music to become a generic, prepackaged product. Haley discussed the situation with *American Songwriter* magazine.

As a musician growing up where I came from, the pinnacle of [a] *music career, from my perspective, was to get a record deal. The first illusion of the*

Cas Haley performing at Red Rocks in Colorado. *Photograph courtesy of Cas Haley.*

music business is that is what you're striving for. Everything that I thought I wanted, when I had it and it was there, it was not anything like I thought. I just wasn't feeling it, it was weird. The first major thing was that my songwriting wasn't going to be part of the album.

They wanted me to go write with people I didn't know. I understand that on a tune or two, but the whole album. I'm no Ashlee Simpson; you know what I'm saying? That totally took away the whole reason for me doing it. For me, it needs to be an honest expression. Even if I'm covering someone's tune, I have to be able to do it in a way I can truly feel it.

I just didn't like the way the whole thing was structured. I felt like I was getting a job. It was one that paid really well but I was going to have bosses. The reason I went into music was to not have a boss; to not feel like I'm working for somebody else.[88]

In 2008, Haley released a self-titled, independent album. The album was a success both commercially and critically. By the end of the year, Billboard had the album ranked no. 8 in the top-selling reggae albums category.

In the ensuing years, Haley released five additional albums. The three most recent albums were released with Jimmy Buffett's Mailboat Records. Another huge highlight for Haley was winning the Lincoln Motor Company's

"Chart Your Course" songwriting competition in 2020. His song "Every Road I'm On" prevailed over 1,600 other entries.

The winning song was written by Haley and his wife, Cassy. For Cas Haley, music is a family affair. The Haleys live the Ohana spirit (the Hawaiian values of love, support and mutual care), with the whole family joining Cas on tour. His wife, Cassy, is his main songwriting partner; his son, Even, is the band's bass player; and his daughter, Nolah, is the band's fiddle player.

So, how did the East Texas reggae star become a ukulele player? It was in Hawaii that Haley first became enamored with the little four-string instruments. In 2010, Haley was invited to tour Hawaii with American reggae singer-songwriter Josh Heinrichs.

I started playing ukulele around 2010, and it stemmed from a trip to Hawaii where I was guest at the Nā Hōkū Hanohano Awards. I met a man named Joe Souza, who happened to own a boutique ukulele company called KANILE'A; he gave me a uke on that trip, and the rest is history. Little did I know at the time that Joe happened to be one of the best uke builders on [the] island, and his instruments are world class. First song was probably one of mine…"La Dah."

I love Hawaii. Some of the best people I have met anywhere. Very beautiful culture with a very grounded presence. And music is a huge part of their culture. That's one of the first thing I noticed, musical performances were everywhere and everyone I met could sing.…The crowds were great.… It's like having a big choir cause they sing.

I think there is something very special about the uke. The uke is very gentle and accessible and it brings a completely different energy to a song. I even feel like I sing differently. It's magic.[89]

Debbie Porter

Wandering through Half Price Books is always an adventure in discovery. It's place to find a hidden gem one was previously unaware of, especially in the CD section. So, what have we found today?

This Is Ukulele Country by Deb Porter. The cover is striking, a collection of ukuleles among the Texas bluebonnets. The songs are familiar, a collection of mainly familiar country standards, such as "Hey Good Lookin'," "Act Naturally," "I Fall to Pieces" and "Tennessee Waltz," along with an original by Deb "Debbie" Porter, "Louisiana Girl." Some of the musicians on the recording are also familiar: the legendary Lloyd Maines on steel guitar and the incomparable Pops Bayless and Austin Ukulele Society founder Bob Guz on ukulele.

But what about Deb Porter? I had heard her name in ukulele circles but wasn't that familiar with her work. I had to ask my friend and expert in all things about the ukulele, Dallas Ukulele Headquarters founder Mark Levine, about her. "Debbie Porter has been a strong member of both the ukulele and dulcimer community for years. "She's a skilled instructor and musician; she's always great to work with or just watch."[90]

Debbie Porter grew up in Northeast Texas and began playing ukulele at the age of eleven. When she was sixteen, her mother saved enough S&H Green Stamps (if this strikes a memory, you are showing your age) to buy Debbie a Kay banjo. When the banjo arrived, Debbie immediately tuned it to sound like a ukulele.

Deborah Porter displaying her CD with Noel Tardy at the Lone Star Uke Fest in 2012.
Photograph courtesy of Dallas Ukulele Headquarters.

In 1971, she moved to Austin. Debbie studied drama at St. Edwards University, and she found herself immersed in the Austin singer-songwriter culture. Debbie got to perform at legendary clubs like the Chequered Flag, which was owned by Kerrville Folk Fest founder, Rod Kennedy.

In 1974, she met the love of her life. However, tragedy struck in 1978, when her husband suffered a traumatic brain injury in a car wreck. For years, Debbie had been writing love songs for him on her acoustic guitar. After his injury, she was unable to pick up a guitar for six years.

But like the mythical phoenix, a new musical direction rose from the ashes of tragedy.

> *So I pulled this guitar out and when I started playing it I just immediately started weeping I couldn't play the guitar anymore. It was so tied up with the loss and the trauma that we had gone through and I thought I just I can't play. Shortly after that by weird coincidence I met a guy, a little slight dude from Texas named David Schnaufer up in Mountain View*

Arkansas at the Folk Center. He started playing this little dulcimer that you just needed one finger to go up and down on the melody string and make this beautiful music. I did not have any former emotional ties to this instrument and I was a singer and I loved music. I just fell into it. I mean it was just stunning and I fell into a beautiful friendship with David Schnaufer. He used to come stay with Richard and I and spend Christmases with us. He was just a very giving person. I saw how he taught. I just thought what a gift this instrument has been, so I started playing. He started inviting me on stage and then other people started inviting me to festivals and it was just wonderful.[91]

Debbie was confronted with another personal tragedy in 2006, when David Schnaufer passed away. Once again, Debbie was able to find the light in this dark time. She created the Dulcimers for David project. It was a way to keep his memory alive through a project that would get mountain dulcimers in the hands of as many children as possible.

Through the years, Debbie has been a popular instructor at festivals and events across the country, teaching ukulele, dulcimer and vocals. A sampling

Dirje A. Childs of the Wahooligans (*right*) and Deborah Porter at Bath House Cultural Center in Dallas, Texas, in 2012. *Photograph courtesy of Dallas Ukulele Headquarters.*

of these events and festivals include the Quarantunes Virtual Dulcimer Festivals, an Austin Ukulele Society Workshop, the Winter Festival of Acoustic Music, the Lone Star Ukulele Festival, the Winter Creek Reunion, the Lagniappe Dulcimer Festival, the Mardi Gras Dulcimer Festival, the Western Carolina Dulcimer Week and the Midwest Uke Fest.

Debbie is a prolific musician and instructor, having released multiple albums, instructional DVDs and tablature books for both ukulele and dulcimer. Through music, she has been able to not only uplift herself but also positively impact thousands of others, much like her friend and mentor, David Schnaufer.

17
The Lori Sealy Concept

The 2024 Lubbock Arts Fair was dubbed "Colorama." One of the musical acts at the fair took that word to heart. Lori Sealy, with her ukulele slung low like she was a member of ZZ Top, strode on stage in a dress that could have been designed by Jackson Pollock and Prince. She topped off the look with a multicolored wig and a painter's palette for a hat. The fair attendees were in for quite a show.

Lori was born in Jacksonville, Florida, and grew up a navy brat. She lived in California and Virginia before her father retired and the family moved to Snyder, Texas, to help care for her grandmother. While living in Virginia, the Easter bunny brought her a keyboard. Lori taught herself to read music and played every song in the two books that came with keyboard.

Lori was a 1987 graduate of Hardin-Simmons University. Piano was her whole world. She was a piano major all throughout college but quickly realized she needed a degree that could guarantee her a job, so she went into elementary education. Lori has a general education bachelor's degree and certifications in early childhood and elementary music. Her ukulele career started a few decades after her graduation.

I didn't pick up a uke until my band had a TTU (Texas Tech University) Hawaiian gig back in 2008. My first was a Martin, but I prefer the Cordoba cutaway. I have ten-plus ukes, some bought, most gifted. The uke I use at gigs was gifted to me by the niece of Buddy Holly, Ingrid Holly Kaiter. I named her Cricket in honor of Buddy Holly and the Crickets.

Above: Lori Sealy, with Kurt Melle on bass, performing at the Lubbock Arts Festival. *Photograph from the Jeff Campbell collection.*

Right: Lori Sealy performing at the Lubbock Arts Festival. *Photograph from the Jeff Campbell collection.*

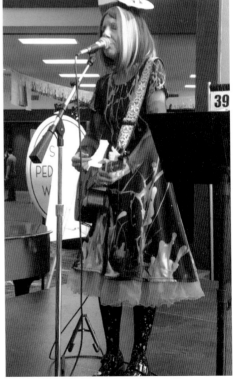

I've been performing live with the uke for about sixteen years. Sure is easier than lugging the big keyboard around! I used to perform eight to ten shows a month when I lived in Lubbock, playing festivals, private parties and retirement homes. Now I play the Lubbock Pancake Festival, the Lubbock Arts Festival and many shows for various events in my hometown of Snyder, Texas. Playing in Snyder is my favorite![92]

So, how did the low slung ukulele stance come about? "I sling my ukes low because I am a rocker! Plus I can see it better. I held it higher when I weighed ninety pounds more, but as I lost weight, the uke was dropping so I just slung it low, and I love it."[93]

Lori also plays some of her chords with her thumb over the top of the neck. What's up with that? "I do the thumb over because I have what I call 'funky thumbs.' They are double jointed, and I can't bend my thumb behind the neck. I just played it like I wanted, then found out lots of folks do it. Trying to follow me at a jam can be confusing."[94]

Bass player Kurt Melle has no problem following Lori.

Kurt Melle has been Lori's music collaborator for decades. Kurt studied electric bass and upright bass at South Plains College in Levelland, Texas. Kurt left the Levelland College with a degree in commercial music with an emphasis in country and bluegrass. Originally from Colorado, Kurt spent his formative years playing trombone and tuba.

Lori played with Kurt in the duo Easy Does It. The two of them also had a couple of fiddle bands, Midnight on the Water, with triple fiddles, keyboard, bass and guitar, and TripleShot, with one fiddle, keys, bass and guitar.

LSC (The Lori Sealy Concept) started in 2013, after the duo with Kurt fizzled out. We played mostly western swing and oldies. I wanted to play songs from my childhood. I have a little collection of 45s and I play a lot of those tunes…"Rockin' Robin," "These Boots are Made for Walking," etc. The "concept" is that I welcome musicians to join me. My audience gets to hear them, and their audience gets to hear me, and jamming is always fun. I hire Kurt Melle to play bass for me for the bigger events.

I play washboard, too. Her name is Hazel, like the maid from the TV show. The brand is Maid-Rite, so I had to choose a maid name, and it had to be Hazel. We've played the Pancake Festival fifteen years and the Arts Festival around thirteen years. I'm an eccentric dresser, so I really love dressing for whatever the theme is. We're known as "Flapjax" when we play the Pancake Festival.[95]

Lori is also a full-time teacher in Snyder, Texas. She teaches twelve classes a day, including pre-K through fourth grade and fifth grade choir. "I teach my students keyboard and some ukulele. We just got a keyboard lab and are having a ball with that. Music class is always fun and never boring."[96]

If you go see LSC, bring your ukulele, you may have the chance to jam with Lori and Kurt. However, if you don't have a ukulele or another musical instrument, Lori may let you play Hazel the washboard!

18

The Wahooligans and
David "Hambone" Hendley

avid Hendley started playing guitar in 1961. He was ten years old and wanted to emulate his eighteen-year-old brother. David's brother had started college, and it looked like he was having a great time playing guitar. On a spring break trip to Mexico, his brother picked up a guitar for David at a street market. For David, there was no looking back.

David's guitar journey coincided with the American folk music revival. David's playing was influenced by the folk artists of the day and the folk music television show *Hootenanny*. "My best friend from down the street and I would spend endless hours practicing and playing. Our first performance was at the end-of-the-year assembly at our elementary school in 1961. We played Woody Guthrie's 'This Land Is Your Land' and another song I can't remember. A crowd of well over two hundred for our first performance!"[97]

However, four lads from Liverpool would lead David and thousands of other kids away from the folk scene. Tom Petty talked about The Beatles' February 9, 1964 performance on the *Ed Sullivan Show*, "I think the whole world was watching that night. It certainly felt that way—you just knew it, sitting in your living room, that everything around you was changing. It was like going from black-and-white to color. Really."[98]

If David Hendley had a guitar interest before, he now had a guitar obsession. He was determined to get an electric guitar and start a band. By high school, David and his friends had formed a rock band. "By our last year of school, we were getting gigs semiregularly. In truth, we were not very good, simply playing whatever was popular on the radio at the time, but we were seventeen and the fourteen-year-olds thought we were cool and would hire us to play at their parties."[99]

After graduation, the David Hendley electric guitar era would end. Living in a college dorm, he was unable to play an electric guitar with a big amp. David also had little interest in starting a new band in a new city. After college, David met his future wife, who loved to sing. So, David picked up the acoustic guitar again. The couple played and sang for their personal enjoyment. Eventually, with another friend, David formed an acoustic trio and enjoyed a successful ten-year run playing at coffeehouses and listening rooms.

In 2005, a longtime friend, John Smith, told Dave he wanted to start a vaudeville-style band and asked if Dave would be interested in joining. John had a gift of showmanship, character

The singer-songwriter, ukulele strummer, ceramic artist (we could call him a potter, but folks may take that the wrong way) David "Hambone" Hendley. *Photograph courtesy of David Hendley.*

creation and costume design. John was an experienced old-time medicine show performer who reveled in being the snake oil salesman. At the time, Dave was playing a repertoire of 1930s–1940s songs. So, the band seemed like a good fit for him. John's wife, Dirje, was an exceptional cellist, but she agreed to join this vaudevillian band to play banjo.

This was the beginning of The Wahooligans. The band name was taken from a song written by Cliff Friend, "Wah-Hoo," which was recorded by the Hoosier Hotshots in 1936. "Wah-Hoo" was the first song the band learned as a group. They all loved the idea of combining "Wah-Hoo" and "Hooligans" for the band's name. All three came up with vaudevillian names for the band, "Hambone Hendley" for David Hendley, "JB Wahoo" for John Smith and "Dirje Faye Wahoo" for Dirje Smith.

David started out playing guitar in the band, but one day, John handed him a baritone ukulele and said, "Here, try this." Since it was an entry-level instrument, David didn't know if John brought it to fool around with or if it was specifically for David. However, that little baritone ukulele would propel David's musicianship in a new and fruitful direction.

The Wahooligans. *Photograph courtesy of David Hendley.*

Wow, what a revelation! It ignited a sustained period of creativity and enthusiasm and a new understanding of music theory. Diminished, augmented and "passing" chords are of course common in jazz-oriented songs, but they are difficult to play on the guitar (for me anyway) and involve muting various strings and some long finger stretches. With only four strings on the ukulele instead of six on the guitar, these chords become simple to play! I started writing songs with twelve or more chords, some with as many as twenty chords, thanks to all the passing and diminished chords. Since a baritone ukulele is tuned exactly the same as the four highest strings on a guitar, I was quite familiar with where the notes fell on the fret board. But I quickly discovered that, to sound their best, chord fingerings or "voicings" were different on a ukulele compared to standard guitar chords. Combine that with nylon strings rather than steel strings and more interesting and distinctive sounds can be fashioned on the baritone ukulele.[100]

David was all in on the ukulele and eventually bought a better-quality baritone ukulele. As his friends saw him playing a ukulele, they started giving him ukuleles. At one time, he had four baritone ukuleles. He was able to pass a few on to interested friends and is now down to two. He also bought a concert ukulele for his wife, just for fun. As it turned out, she didn't really do much with it, so David started playing it, wrote a couple of songs with it and began taking it to gigs. "Great gift, huh? Like the husband who gives his wife a power drill for their wedding anniversary."[101]

> *After six or seven good years The Wahooligans disbanded. "I hate it, as those were some of the best times of my life. My favorite concerts as a Wahooligan were the several Lone Star Ukulele Festivals in Dallas we played at, organized by the late Noel Tardy. A hundred and fifty enthusiastic ukulele players together for workshops and concerts for two whole days!"*[102]

David continued to play and perform, not as much as he did when he was with the band, but he was still scoring the occasional gig. He had five or six songs written for The Wahooligans that were never properly recorded, so in 2016, he recorded and released a solo album as David Hambone Hendley.

The Wahooligans perform at the 2012 Lone Star Uke Fest. *Photograph courtesy of Dallas Ukulele Headquarters.*

David has been a professional potter for almost fifty years, so also included on the CD are several songs he wrote for or about potters.

Today, David mostly plays the baritone ukulele. Probably as a result of playing guitar for so many years, David likes having that bass string to anchor the sound. "[By the way], I pronounce it 'you-ka-lay-lee,' not 'ook-koo-leh-leh,' as I'm told is the proper Hawaiian pronunciation. That just seems pretentious to a Texan like me."[103] Spoken like a true Texan!

When David travels to teach pottery workshops, he always takes his guitar and ukuleles to entertain the students during breaks or in the evening. For David, writing and playing music and making pottery, while both creative, are very different. A different part of the brain is utilized. When working with clay, his mind can drift and meander in any direction. When working, he usually listens to music (all genres) or podcasts and can give them his full attention. His hands just kind of know what to do with the clay. When he is writing or rehearsing music, however, he needs to concentrate, and this requires quiet and no distractions.

So, what does the future hold for David "Hambone" Hendley? "I'll probably continue with music and the ukulele, as well as with pottery making, as long as I'm able. It has become an expected tradition that I write and perform a song for my every-five-year high school reunions. I recently performed the fourth such song, and the next one in a few years will be the fifth. My imminent next project, at my daughter's request, is to write and perform a song for her upcoming wedding. Not an easy order. Need to get started on that!"[104]

19

Texans and Their Ukuleles

ALEXANDER BEGGINS

Alexander Beggins, his friends call him Zandi, is one half of the indie pop duo Wild Child. Wild Child was formed in 2010 with Zandi on vocals and baritone ukulele and Kelsey Wilson on vocals and violin.

Zandi fell in love with ukuleles as a teenager and has played them in bands ever since. The Austin-based musician has also created a side project titled CoCo Zandi. The project puts a modern spin on 1950s Hawaiian music, blending baritone ukulele steel drums, three female backup singers and a dash of electronic percussion. Coco Zandi released the album *As Simple as a Dream* in 2021.

FRANK BURKETT

Frank Burkett passed away on September 23, 2018, at the age of eighty-nine. To say he led a full life is quite an understatement. Professionally, he was known as Fort Worth's premiere ad man.

> *His output is legendary. His "Fort Worth National…that's MY bank!" jingle put Witherspoon on the map. He did wonderful consumer work for Texas Electric Service Co. and equally good—if not as visible—industrial advertising for the likes of Hobbs Trailers and Power Service Products.*

Even in his "retirement" he found a way to apply his natural talents, scripting the Fort Worth Stock Show tribute vignette performed at every rodeo performance during its 1996 centennial celebration. Additionally, for the October 2001 grand opening of Central Market, he penned original lyrics to a Grateful Dead tune that store executives performed at the event. [105]

He also played piano, taught Sunday school and sang in the church choir. Often, he picked up trash, bottles and cans on his walks through the west side of Fort Worth. Burkett drove a 1966 Mustang convertible around Fort Worth for more than forty years. He was also a runner, canoeist, songwriter, skier and tennis player.

Burkett, along with his wife, Sue, hosted a sing-along on the eve of the Fourth of July for forty years. Last but not least, he also played the baritone ukulele.

Elizabeth Burns

Elizabeth Burns is a teacher with over twenty years of experience. Her passion is music, and she has used bucket drums, drum circles and the recorder to show students the joy of making music.

In 2018, through the Abilene Education Foundation, Elizabeth received a STAR grant (Strategies for Teaching, Assessment and Retention) to purchase ukuleles. "My goal for the ukulele is to create a curiosity for playing other string instruments such as the guitar and to give them a love for playing instruments," she said. [106]

First, Elizabeth taught her students the ukulele's history and the parts of the ukulele. Then the students learned a song on their very first day!

According to Kale Fried, a fifth grader, "On the first day, Mrs. Burns taught us the C chord and we played 'Put a Lime in the Coconut.'" [107]

Mrs. Burns learned to play the ukulele in the fourth grade at Jackson Elementary in Abilene. Now, she is passing on her ukulele knowledge to a new generation.

Roy T. Cone

Roy T. Cone (he says the T stands for Trouble) learned to build ukuleles while he was part of a ukulele club in Seabrook, Texas. It was one of the earliest ukulele clubs in the United States, along with the Vokuleles of Chico, California.

Roy got in the ukulele business in the 1950s and eventually started Ukulele World in Seabrook (between Galveston and Houston). The store was one of the first online retailers of ukuleles and ukulele accessories. Roy built the "Tuma Vita," which was inspired by the Roy Smeck Vita Uke. Tuma stood for "Texas ukulele manufacturers association."

In 1994, Roy joined the Houston University Baptist Church Ukulele Band. In 1995, he talked to the New Braunfels Herald Zeitung about one of their shows:

> 'The most important gig we played last year was at the Texas Prison System. It took us longer to get in and out than it did to play.'
>
> — Roy Cone

A Roy Cone quote. *From the* New Braunfels Herald-Zeitung, *May 14, 1995, www.newspapers.com.*

"The most important gig we played last year was at the Texas prison system. It took us longer to get in and out than it did to play."[108]

In 2011, Roy talked about his love for the ukulele, "It's a happy instrument that makes you smile and feel good," attests Cone, who says he sold "hundreds" of instruments over the past year. "Hell, I'm 84, so anything that makes me feel good at my age is bound to not be too bad."[109]

Logan Daffron

Around 2000, Logan Daffron was one of the early participants in Mark Levine's jams at the Dallas Half Price Bookstore. He met Mark while teaching a class at the same time of the jam—a class on juggling!

A professional juggler, Logan has played at parties, opened concerts for artists like Melissa Etheridge & Leon Redbone and taught juggling classes. He also served as an instructor to the Dallas Cowboys football team, helping the NFL gladiators with their hand-eye coordination.

> *Now, juggling can be a lot of fun; play with skill and play with space, play with rhythm.*
>
> —*Juggler Michael Moschen*[110]

Does juggling make playing ukulele easy? Well, for Logan, his previous guitar experience was a big plus. Most of the chord shapes are the same for

Two musicians, Del Ray and Logan Daffron, on a double ukulele in 2011. *Photograph courtesy of Dallas Ukulele Headquarters.*

ukulele and guitar. As a guitar player, Logan had always wanted to learn to build guitars. With his newfound ukulele enthusiasm, he decided to learn to build ukuleles.

When a two-week intensive ukulele-building course in Hawaii landed in his lap, Daffron jumped at the chance. "I had always wanted to build an acoustic guitar, but there was nowhere to learn," he laughs. "It seemed like a good reason to go to Hawaii without having to get married."[111]

Logan started building ukuleles in the garage of his east Dallas home. His customer base grew, with one of his most famous customers being Dallasite Edie Brickell of Edie Brickell and the New Bohemians. By the way, Edie's husband is Paul Simon. Yes, that Paul Simon, who also happens to be a juggler.

Joyce Flaugher

Joyce Flaugher resides in Rockport, Texas. However, she was once the ukulele ambassador of San Antonio.

During her husband's naval tour of duty in Hawaii, Joyce learned to hula dance. In the late 1970s, when the couple returned to Texas, Joyce began dancing for a Houston ukulele group. Joyce remembers when her ukulele playing started: "During the times when they didn't need me to dance, I just picked up the ukulele and learned to play it," Flaugher said. "It was just so much fun and so easy to do and everybody always had a good time. It's a very social instrument."[112]

Joyce started teaching ukulele in 1985. During her time in San Antonio, Joyce spearheaded sponsors for the city's ukulele festival. She also led the monthly ukulele jam at the Lions Field Adult and Senior Citizens Center. Plus, she performed with two San Antonio ukulele bands, the Ladies and Gents and Pearl's Girls.

Chelle Graham

Chelle Graham is the lead singer and ukulele player for the band The She. The Richardson, Texas–based band was formed in 2021. The other members of the trio are Tyler Shepherd on bass and Justin Garison on drums and percussion.

The She play a mixture of diverse covers and originals in the North Texas area. The trio released their first extended play recording in 2023.

Adolph Hofner

The late, great Waylon Jennings said, "Once you're down in Texas, Bob Wills is still the King." Bob Wills (1905–1975) is known as the king of western swing. Think of western swing as cowboy jazz, a dance music melting pot of fiddle tunes, swing, Dixieland jazz, blues, country, western and old-time string bands.

Opposite: Joyce Flaugher at the 2008 San Antonio Uke Fest. *Photograph courtesy of Dallas Ukulele Headquarters.*

Above: The She perform a holiday concert at Klyde Warren Park in Dallas, Texas, in 2021. *Photograph from the Jeff Campbell collection.*

Right: Adolph Hofner record. *Internet Archive.*

One of the most prominent western swing bandleaders was Adolph Hofner (1916–2000). His early years were spent on the family farm in Lavaca County, Texas. Adolph and his brother, Bash, were greatly influenced by the Czech and German schottisches and polka music in their community. Later in his career, Adolph performed Czech and German music, in addition to western swing.

By Adolph's teen years, the Hofner family had moved to San Antonio. Here, the brothers were influenced by Hawaiian music. Bash became a master of the steel guitar, while Adolph evolved into a vocalist in the Bing Crosby style. "Then we got a little trio started, we called ourselves the Hawaiian Serenaders. Simon Garcia he played ukulele, Bash played steel and I played standard but we built up our knowledge of songs and things went.…You learn more songs; but we more or less stayed with the Hawaiian and the popular."[113]

Revisiting those early days in South Texas, the brothers started their musical journey on a single ukulele. Like most folks of the era, they ordered their ukulele from a catalog. It would not have been economically feasible for a farm family to order two ukuleles. "So me and my brother finally ordered one and I had to broke it before we got to the house, it was a ukulele. Me and my brother Bash, we been in this business, him and I neck to neck forever.[114]

JOHN DRISKELL HOPKINS

John Driskell Hopkins was born in San Antonio on May 3, 1971, and raised in North Georgia. The talented multi-instrumentalist is best known as a founding member of the Zach Brown Band.

Hopkins has also collaborated with the Jerry Douglas, along with the bluegrass bands Balsam Range and the Dappled Grays. He also performs with his own John Driskell Hopkins Band. He is proficient on banjo, guitar, electric bass, upright bass and ukulele.

So, how did Hopkins become a ukulele player? He talked about it in a 2017 interview with Kala Ukuleles. "I've had a ukulele for a long time, I only started using one in our shows in the past 5 or 6 years. It's a great complement to Zac's nylon string [guitar] and it's really wonderful on the beach songs we play. I also like it when we do an acoustic set. It's cool to have a different voicing when there are so many guitars on stage."[115]

During the holiday season of 2021, Hopkins was diagnosed with ALS (amyotrophic lateral sclerosis). He did not go public with the diagnosis until

May 2022. Hopkins made the announcement on YouTube, his Zach Brown Band brothers standing by his side. Hopkins started the Hop On a Cure foundation to fund research, prevention and reversal of the disease.

Kainoa Kamaka

San Antonio, the Alamo city, is the home of mariachis, Tex-Mex food, the San Antonio Spurs, the River Walk and the "ambassador of aloha"? Kainoa Kamaka was born on the big island of Hawaii in 1970 but now resides in San Antonio. He was dubbed the ambassador of aloha by the lieutenant governor of Hawaii.

San Antonio is a military town, and one of Kainoa's cousins was stationed in San Antonio. While visiting his cousin, Kai fell in love with old San Antone. He would visit San Antonio as much as possible over the next few years before finally relocating.

Kainoa is a descendant of a talented musical family. His father is a musician, and his mother is a hula dancer. His uncles were members of one of Hawaii's most famous and popular bands, Hui Ohana. The trio, Ledward and Nedward Kalapana and Dennis Pavao, captivated Hawaiian music listeners in 1972. During a Hawaiian renaissance of sorts, Hui Ohana brought the attractive sounds of male falsetto singing and slack key guitar to a new generation. While still in Hawaii, Kainoa started the band Kainoa Ohana, in which he sang and played the ukulele.

Presently, Kainoa travels across South Texas, serenading Texans with his voice and ukulele. He performs at senior living communities, presents Aloha Friday at the L&L Hawaiian BBQ in San Antonio and is also a "winter Texan entertainer" entertaining across the Rio Grande Valley from January to March.

Tom Mcdermott

A guitar, ukulele, hurdy gurdy, theremin, bodhran, lyre, flute and drums—sounds like a band right? In most cases, it would be. However, for this tale, these are all the instruments played by Tom Mcdermott.

Tom is a graduate of Texas Christian University's Brite Divinity School and has a Bachelor of Arts degree from the University of Texas at Austin. A natural storyteller, he, in 1991, began entertaining kids from "one to ninety two" across the United States and in Ireland. His goal was not just to entertain but also to motivate, while inspiring creativity and critical thinking.

A modern-day minstrel, Tom has been recognized for his craft over the years. Tom was awarded first place in the National Irish Storytelling Contest. Tom also received the John Henry Faulk Award for his excellence and contributions in storytelling.

The former president of the Tejas Storytelling Association has also released two albums of his songs and stories. Tom is also a former social worker with Austin Planned Parenthood and the Tarrant Area Drug Rehab Institute.

Tom is an ordained United Methodist minister at the First United Methodist Church in Fort Worth, Texas.

PHIL MORRIS

At the age of seven, Phil Morris fell in love with ukuleles. "I probably didn't play any song at all. I just strummed it all of the time. I wasn't old and smart enough to play proper songs, but I really loved that thing," Morris recalled. "To hold that instrument and hear the sound of the string was really something."[116]

Morris, who lives in Garland, Texas, was attending a Luthiers Interactive of North Texas meeting when he met Dan Folbert. The two luthiers bonded over their shared passion for ukuleles.[117] Around 2007, the pair started hand building banjo-ukuleles under the name of Spanky's Banjo Ukes.

The banjo ukulele is a four-string ukulele with a banjo body. It plays like a ukulele but sounds like a banjo.

Lisa "Miz" Markley is a jazz vocalist, composer and songwriter. She played a Spanky uke while performing the song "Velvet Divan." "I love, love, love Spanky ukes. Sadly, I do not own one myself. Phil [Mr. Spanky Uke himself] loaned me the beautiful Spanky uke I played in that video [performance of 'Velvet Divan']. I hope someday to own one if I can get Phil to make one before he retires. What I love

Opposite: A beautiful Spank Uke. *Photograph courtesy of Ukulele Underground.*

Above: Spanky Ukes's booth at the Lone Star Uke Fest. *Photograph courtesy of Dallas Ukulele Headquarters.*

about the Spankys is that the back cover is easily removed, so it can be an open-back. They are beautifully crafted, too."[118]

If you're thinking of buying a Spanky banjo-uke, it's going to take more than your pocket change. Used listings on the Ukulele Underground website are in the $900 to $975 range!

JACK PEPPER

Jack Pepper, not to be confused with pepper jack, was a vaudeville star and ukulele player. Pepper was born on June 14, 1902, in Palestine, Texas. Pepper's singing style and ukulele techniques were similar to those of Cliff Edwards. Pepper was also quite a comedian and dancer. Pepper's vaudeville career started in his adolescent years when he performed with his sisters. By the 1920s, he was a starring in a duo with Frank Salt, appropriately named Salt and Pepper.

Pepper is probably most famous for rubbing elbows with the famous. He was Ginger Rogers's first of many husbands. Though they were married only two years, they did have an act together called Ginger and Pepper. Pepper was also good friends with Bing Crosby, Bob Hope and Will Rogers. Pepper passed away at the age of seventy-six in Los Angeles.

KEVIN RUSSELL

Born and raised in Beaumont, Texas, Kevin Russell started his musical adventure at the age of fourteen. That's when he discovered his father's guitar under a bed. In 1985, he started his first band, the Picket Line Coyotes, in Shreveport, Louisiana. After a few years, the Coyotes headed to Dallas and the bright lights of Deep Ellum. Then they traveled down I-35 to try their luck in Austin. In Austin, the band began to unravel.

Kevin started a new band, the Grackles (if you've been to Austin, you know how appropriate that name is). The Grackles morphed into the Gourds. Starting in 1994, the band stayed together until 2003. During those nineteen years, the band recorded eleven albums. The band's claim to fame was a bluegrass-infused cover of Snoop Dog's "Gin and Juice."

When the band went on hiatus, Kevin started a side project, Shinyribs. The Shinyribs side project has grown into a full-time touring band. Kevin calls the band's music "country-soul" and "swamp-funk."[119] In his shows, Kevin plays guitar and a ukulele.

His ukulele of choice is a six-string Mele mahogany tenor. On this particular ukulele, the C and the A strings are doubled, similar to a mandolin. Kevin also uses the ukulele for recording sessions.

Kevin covered "If You Don't Know Me by Now" (the original was recorded by Harold Melvin & the Blue Notes in 1972) for the Shinyribs album *Gulf Coast Museum*.

The producer, George Reiff, that was his choice of song. I'm always learning songs on the ukulele, and that was one I'd been playing with because…it's such a cool song. On our first record, we did "A Change Is Going to Come" at the end…and for the second record, we wanted to do the same thing—a classic soul song. That's one of the greatest ones of all time. It's a surprising song to hear just on the ukulele. Most versions are pretty orchestral, lots of production on them. To hear that song stripped down, just me and the ukulele and Brandy [Zdan] singing harmony, I thought that was a really cool effect and surprising. It shows what a great song it is. Really, if a song's good, it can stand on its own like that.[120]

If Shinyribs comes to your town, go and experience some swamp-funk music played on a ukulele.

WASHTUB JERRY

Washtub Jerry resides in Fort Davis, Texas. The name "Washtub" come from Jerry's proficiency on the washtub bass. A washtub bass is a one-string instrument that uses a washtub as its resonator. The string is attached to a wooden stick. The washtub bass player can change the note by adjusting the string tension by bowing the stick. Jerry's washtub is from a town in Mexico where the zinc coating produces the sound he's looking for. The string he uses is the clutch cable from a Porche, and he wears leather gloves to pluck the string.

Jerry has backed up a multitude of musicians over the years. He is a member of the International Society of Bassists, and in 2013, he received an American Cowboy Culture Association Award for western music. Jerry is also an experienced ukulele player. In fact, he can play the ukulele and washtub bass at the same time. "I perform on the ukulele and washtub bass simultaneously. I am not a solo act, so I am backing my music partner. The two of us can produce a four-person sound which the audience enjoys."[121]

Like many ukulele players, Jerry had two incidents that led him to the ukelele, frustration with the guitar and a trip to Hawaii.

> *A man, Tom, came to our house in the early 1950s to ask my dad for a loan to purchase a car. Tom brought a guitar and played a song or two— one must have been a blues song that really caught my ear. I had never seen a guitar, but noticed there were six strings, but his left hand had only four fingers plus one apposing thumb. My first thought was, "There's a serious problem here." My second thought was, "I really like the sound of the multiple strings." I later learned that those were called chords. I spent the next handful of years looking for a way to play chords but could not play one of those six-stringed instruments. I believe I was in college when someone mentioned to me that I should look into a ukulele because they had only four strings. I'd never heard of a ukulele.*
>
> *Growing up in Alamogordo, New Mexico, I had no idea what a ukulele was. A couple years later, I was a work-study student at New Mexico State University. During my second job phase, a fellow student, Stretch, and I were wandering around Honolulu, Hawaii, killing time to catch the next plane to Eniwetok Island to doppler-shift track satellites. We came upon a music store that was selling a ukulele for $5.00. We discussed this major investment for a while and decided to each put up $2.50. This was in 1963. I also bought several books that showed how to form various chords.*

I soon learned that a ukulele was exactly what I had been looking for all those years. (In spite of playing bassoon and accordion in junior high and high school.) I sold my half interest in the ukulele to Stretch for $1.00 and bought a $10.00 ukulele on our next trip through Honolulu.

Jerry has authored and published four books, including two on ukulele, *Neck Anywhere* and *Neck Anywhere, Lefty*. Jerry talks about how the books came about.

After learning a few ukulele chords, I became aware that most people want to play songs. Instead, my goal from the get-go was to be able to play rhythm chords in any key anywhere on the neck so that I could accompany lead musicians. I wrote a course of action to learn chords in a meaningful order and in "neighborhood" groups. It worked! After completing my ukulele course, I was able to perform with other musicians. I had launched my adult music career. Years later, it dawned on me that other people could benefit from my course, so I had it printed. I have taught many people my "Neck Anywhere!" course and have sold many of my books.

Jerry has collaborated with numerous western artists and with the Midland-Odessa Symphony Orchestra. Jerry teamed up with New Mexico cowboy Sid Hausman on the albums *Blue Horizon* and *Colorado Belle*. With Sid on vocals and baritone ukulele, Jerry played the ukulele and washtub bass simultaneously. On some tracks, Sid played banjo or dobro while Jerry played ukulele.

Jerry worked with Bruce Newman on the album *Cajun Cowboys*. Bruce performs on guitar and banjo-guitar while Jerry plays ukulele and washtub bass. Jerry has also recorded with Al "Doc" Mehl, Jeff Gore, Bill Chappell and fiddler Glenn Moreland.

Washtub Jerry performs at many of the cowboy poetry and music events in Texas and across the West. It would be worth the price of admission to see a man play bass and ukulele at the same time!

20

Tiny Tim's Texas Revival

Tiny Tim was the very definition of a "one hit wonder." "Tiptoe Through the Tulips" reached no. 17 on the Billboard charts in 1968. After that, only two of his singles made the Hot 100: "Bring Back Those Rockabye Baby Days" at no. 95 in 1968 and "Great Balls of Fire" at no. 85 in 1969. Throughout the 1970s and into the '80s, the novelty of Tiny Tim had worn off. He no longer performed under the big tent, but the circus continued.

Frank Sinatra's Reprise Records, home for artists like Neil Young, dropped him from the label. Tiny Tim started his own record label, Vic Tim Records, a tribute to his wife, Miss Vicki. The label released five unsuccessful singles and then disappeared. He released another unsuccessful single on Scepter Records in 1972. He also recorded for West Germany's Bellaphon Records and Polydor Records in the United Kingdom.

Tiny Tim continued to tour relentlessly across the nation wherever he could land a gig. However, he still was enough of a draw to perform quite a few lucrative dates in Las Vegas.

Australia—and specifically Martin Sharp—provided Tiny Tim with a professional lifeline in 1979 and 1980. Martin Sharp was a Sydney-based pop artist, cartoonist, filmmaker and songwriter. His most recognizable work was with the 1960s blues/rock band Cream (Jack Bruce, Ginger Baker and Eric Clapton). Sharp designed the cover art for two Creem albums (*Wheels of Fire* and *Disraeli Gears*) and wrote the lyrics to one of the band's signature songs, "Tales of Brave Ulysses."

Tiny Tim and Martin Short. *The National Library of Australia, William Yang.*

In 1967, Sharp was in London when he saw Tiny Tim for the first time. "I'd eaten a bit of hash or something, but he just amazed me," Mr. Sharp recalled in the book *Electrical Banana*, "I'd been doing a lot of collage work, like a van Gogh figure within a Magritte landscape. I was fascinated by the language of art, and mixing and connecting things. Tiny was working with songs in a similar way. He had a quickness and breadth of songs that was breathtaking. I knew the language he was using. He was such a modern artist."[122]

Sharp produced three albums for Tiny Tim. Only a handful of copies were pressed of the first two, and they were not released in the United States. Sharp also produced Tiny Tim's Non Stop Luna Park Marathon, a concert at the Sydney amusement park Luna Park. The concert was promoted as an attempt for the world record for the longest nonstop professional singing. Tiny Tim reportedly sang 120 songs in 120 minutes.

Returning to America, Tiny Tim recorded "Tip Toe to the Gas Pumps," a response to the long lines at gas pumps due to the OPEC oil crisis. The circus continued.

In 1982, Tiny Tim met a Dallas musician, promoter, magazine publisher and record store owner, Bucks Burnett. Bucks became Tiny Tim's confidant for the rest of his life. Though their relationship was tumultuous, Tiny Tim considered Bucks his manager.

> *There is no way to bring it back to life, that magic twist of night; the night I met Tiny Tim.*
>
> *It was 1982, September, I think. A Tiny Tim concert was advertised for a now defunct nightclub, Confetti, once located about where Krispy*

*Kreme stands today at Lovers [Lane] and Greenville [Avenue]. I
hadn't thought of him since his heyday in the late '60s, and curiosity got
the best of me.*

*I decided that I must meet him and interview him for BARK, a music
magazine I was publishing at the time. I had already interviewed Chris
Frantz of Talking Heads, and had met a few rock stars by that point, but
the idea of meeting Tiny Tim went beyond rock star to extraterrestrial. I
could not resist.*[123]

Bucks Burnett's eccentricity would be more than a match for Tiny Tim's.
He was an 8-track tape collector, once paying $1,000 for a rare Beatles
8-track.

*I found out there was another Beatles 8-track I didn't have that came out
in 1982.* The Beatles' 20 Greatest Hits. *It was just one of those
cheesy reissues that the company put out, but they made a few copies in the
initial test run and—this is as the 8-track was dying—Capitol decided not
to release it at the last minute. So those prototypes are all there is and it's
widely believed that there are 10 or fewer copies of this particular eight-
track in existence. I found one and that's what the guy wanted, so that's
what I paid.*[124]

Burnett also opened an 8-track tape museum in Dallas, Texas. He owned
14 Records, a record shop that sold 8-track tapes and the devices to play
them on.

Burnett referred to himself as the "Namedropper," as he tried to meet as
many famous musicians as possible. One avenue he used to pursue this was
his fictitious Mr. Ed fan club.

*I actually made up the Mr. Ed fan club in the mid-'70s as an excuse to
talk to Monty Python over the phone. Dallas was the first city in America to
air Monty Python in the mid-'70s on KERA Channel 13. And you know
how they have their pledge drives every three months? Well, they actually
appeared at the Dallas pledge drive and you would phone in your pledge and
somebody from Monty Python would answer and that was the pledge drive
because the show was so instantly popular in Dallas that people would call
in just to see if John Cleese would answer the phone. So I was just in my
teens at the time and Terry Gilliam answered and we talked for a couple
of minutes and he asked me if I wanted to join Channel 13 and just off*

the top of my head I said "No, do you wanna join the Mr. Ed Fan Club?"
I made it up as something ridiculous sounding and he said, "Is that the
horse?" And I said, "Yeah." And so he laughed about it and then he made
a joke with everyone else in Monty Python and that's how it started: with a
joke between me and Terry Gilliam.[125]

For the uninitiated, *Mister Ed* was a television sitcom that aired from 1961 to 1966. The star of the show, Mr. Ed, was a talking horse voiced by actor Allan Lane. The horse's real name was Bamboo Harvester, and his costar was Alan Young. Young played Mr. Ed's owner, the affable, bumbling architect Wilbur Post.

The made-up Mr. Ed fan club morphed into a real fan club. Burnett gave out free memberships to rock stars like Alice Cooper, Eric Clapton, Pete Townsend and Jimmy Page.[126] The pinnacle of the Mr. Ed fan club was the first (and last) Edstock, a musical festival held at the Dallas Bronco Bowl in 1984.[127] The show featured T-Bone Burnett, Joe Ely, the Stardust Cowboy and Tiny Tim. Alan Young even made an appearance. Unfortunately, Bamboo Harvester had passed away in 1970 and was unavailable.

About a month before the show, Burnett brought Tiny Tim to Dallas to record the *Mister Ed* theme song. The recording was sold as a 45-rpm record at Edstock. The *Mister Ed* theme song is up there with the *Batman*, *Gilligan's Island* and the *Addams Family* themes as far as memorable 1960s television theme songs go. If you ever hear these lyrics, they will forever be embedded in your brain!

> *A horse is a horse, of course, of course*
> *And no one can talk to a horse of course*
> *That is, of course, unless the horse is the famous Mr. Ed!*
> *Go right to the source and ask the horse*
> *He'll give you the answer that you'll endorse*
> *He's always on a steady course*
> *Talk to Mr. Ed!*[128]

On a side note, in 1986, an Ohio evangelist, Jim Brown, claimed that the Tiny Tim version of the *Mister Ed* theme contained satanic messages when played backward.

Edstock lost around $20,000, and it also brought about the demise of the Mr. Ed fan club.[129] Burnett then started a new fan club: the Tiny Tim fan club.

Mr. Ed at Edstock

DALLAS (AP) — The Mr. Ed Fan Club, gathering at a Dallas bowling alley, honored the memory of television's famous talking horse and presented an award to featured guest Tiny Tim.

The ukelele-strumming singer's repertoire was greeted with an ovation from the crowd of 400 and won an award as Greatest Performance of the 20th Century."

Among his numbers was a version of the equine TV star's theme song beginning, "A horse is a horse, of course, of course …"

Alan Young, who played straight man to Ed, also was on hand for the Saturday gathering called "Edstock" ("15 years after Woodstock").

Left: Article about "Edstock." *From the* Salina Journal, *July 11, 1984, www.newspapers.com.*

Right: Tiny Tim "One Man Parade" advertisement. *Author's collection.*

Through the rest of the 1980s, Tiny Tim toured and performed at circuses and dinner theaters. He also played the role of Mervin (Marvelous Mervo), a mentally unstable killer clown in the B-grade slasher movie *Blood Harvest*. He also released a country single, "Leave Me Satisfied," for Nashville-based NLT records.

Entering the 1990s, with the help of Burnett, Tiny Tim had a career revival. Tiny Tim released the albums *Songs of an Impotent Troubadour*, *Tiny Tim's Christmas Album*, *Prisoner of Love: A Tribute to Russ Columbo* and *Girl*. *Songs of an Impotent Troubadour* and *Girl* were produced by Burnett.

On July 4, 1994, Burnett filmed a solo performance by Tiny Tim at a private Dallas, Texas Fourth of July party.[130] The VHS tape was made available by mail order to members of the Tiny Tim fan club. Titled *Tiny Tim's One Man Parade*, the forty-five-minute performance is a presentation of both popular and obscure patriotic songs. Though Tiny Tim was seen as a counterculture figure, he was extremely patriotic. The concert was released on DVD in 2021.

Burnett also introduced Tiny Tim to Brave Combo. Brave Combo, from Denton, Texas, has been described as a punk-polka and fusion polka band. Since 1979, they have been known for their quirky arrangements of popular songs. From a cha-cha version of the Rolling Stones' song "Satisfaction" to a polka version of "Purple Haze" by Jimi Hendrix. The thought was that a mesh of Brave Combo's world music experience and Tiny Tim's encyclopedic knowledge of old songs would produce solid gold.

It was decided that Brave Combo would serve as Tiny Tim's backup band. The album took quite a few years to complete. "Tiny Tim and Big Bucks had a falling out," said Brave Combo founder Carl Finch. "They would fix it every now and then and get back together."[131]

The CD titled *Girl* was finally released in 1996. The songs included a cha-cha version of The Beatles' "Hey Jude" and a Vegas crooner version of Led Zeppelin's "Stairway to Heaven." Jimmy Page of Led Zeppelin, after hearing the Tiny Tim version, reportedly said, "Well, this puts an end to that song."[132] The album was released on vinyl for Record Store Day in 2022. Jokes aside, the recording did receive good reviews. Allmusic.com, in ITS review simply stated, "*Girl* is the best Tiny Tim record since the first one."[133]

Unfortunately, this would be Tiny Tim's last album. Tiny Tim passed away from a heart attack on November 30, 1996, in Minneapolis, Minnesota. No matter what one may think of his musicianship or eccentric personality, there's no question that Tiny Tim's popularity brought even greater awareness to the ukulele.

21

Mark Levine and the Dallas Ukulele Headquarters

Mark Levine has always inspired me. He makes learning the ukulele easy and fun. His personality is a big plus in his communication. Such a sense of humor. He is a great teacher!
—Obid Donlin, Leader of the Kanikapila Island Strummers[134]

In 2024, the Dallas Ukulele Headquarters (DUH) had over 2,000 members on their meetup page. Their Facebook group had over 1,300 members. Through the years, there have been many "spin-off" groups formed from DUH, including the Kanikapila Island Strummers, the Opihi Gang, the Baritone Ukulele Group (BUGs) and the DUH Community Ukulele Band (CUBs).

The seed that would blossom into Dallas Ukulele Headquarters was planted back in 1977; the year Mark Lavine received a Roy Smeck ukulele from his father.

For me, it's a story from my childhood involving my father, an old Martin guitar, a campfire, cheap toy ukuleles and a sinking ship.

My father, a music teacher, former member of the United States Navy Band and a trumpet player, certainly wanted to instill musical skills into his children. One day, I was maybe ten, my dad brought home three Roy Smeck ukuleles. These toy ukuleles came in a yellow-checked plastic case and were quite cute. My dad proceeded to get increasingly frustrated trying to tune these beauties. Unfortunately, cheap wood and cheap strings did

Dallas Ukulele Headquarters Picnic, 2013. *Photograph courtesy of Dallas Ukulele Headquarters.*

not make an easy job of it. He eventually gave up and never touched the ukuleles again.

That wasn't the day that sparked my love of the instrument—far from it! Those ukes had a tough road ahead. Mine got battered, and the cute case vanished. I think at some point in youth, it became a weapon in either a fight with my brother or just a temper tantrum. At any rate, whatever eventually happened to my first uke, it developed some holes that weren't supposed to be there, and I have no idea where it is today.

My brother Mike's uke, on the other hand, somehow followed me when I left California and accompanied me on my moves to Colorado and eventually to Texas. Yes, that's right; I nicked my brother's ukulele. I don't think he missed it. In fact, I'm not even sure if he knows the old Roy Smeck I have today is actually his. If he wants it, he can have it back. At any rate, it managed to stay in boxes or in the backs of closets until....

Mid-life crisis. OK, as mid-life crises go, this was pretty mild. But in my mid-thirties, it became very important to me to rediscover my childhood. And that was when that yellow-checked case, nicked from my brother, seemed to come out of the closet and find me. It suddenly became important to me to learn to play the ukulele, not because of that long-ago day when my father failed to tune it, but because of another memory.

We used to camp when I was young—a lot! My childhood included climbing rocks, hiking and trying to catch frogs and lizards. On one memorable trip through South Dakota, I managed to catch a fish with my hands in a lake. For some reason, my mother let me keep the fish in the sink of our camper for the rest of our trip and all the way home, where the fish got to live out the remainder of his life well fed in a fish tank.

What I remember from those days is my dad sitting around the campfire, playing an old Martin guitar and singing campfire songs. I'm sure there were a bunch, but the one that stuck in my memory and followed me through the years was called "Titanic."

That was what came to me when I held that old Roy Smeck ukulele in the depth of my mid-life crisis: I wanted to learn to play "Titanic" on the ukulele to recapture those memories from my youth.

Did it work? Sort of. I can and do play "Titanic," and I did feel a lot of memories return from camping. But the experiences of playing with people, meeting new friends, and enjoying the ukulele together far exceed that very early hope and expectation I had.[135]

There is now some debate as to exactly what year Dallas Ukulele Headquarters got started. In truth, we were just having fun and not really keeping any records. But it's kind of fun to think there is a veneer of mystery and legend about it. The closest I can really get is 1998.

I had just rediscovered the ukulele and wanted to find others who could help me play and play together. At the time, there was virtually no ukulele presence on the internet. Really, the only resource was Jumpin' Jim Beloff, who had a website for his books and Fluke Ukulele. One of the webpages on this site was a message board.

This type of social media is so outdated, I never see it these days, but basically, there was a list of posts from people with no graphics or pictures listed in chronological order. I asked several times about people and activities in the Dallas area and didn't see any replies.

So, eventually, I announced that a ukulele group was forming in Dallas and announced a meeting date and time.

The location I picked was Half Price Books on Northwest Highway— it's still there. Their original location, located across the street, would have been even better. It was an eclectic building with a second story that had floors not level and all kinds of nooks and crannies. They grew too large for that cool little building, but it would have been perfect for an eclectic group of fledgling ukulele players. Instead, their active location was a huge space. I wanted a little smaller space for the group.

They had a small coffee shop, and I figured we could get together there to practice and play. So, I announced my meeting.

At the time, I really didn't have much of a ukulele to work with. I was dragging around a Roy Smeck toy ukulele my brothers and I had gotten when I was ten. At the time, I was about thirty-five. So, the uke was twenty-five years old. On the plus side, even plywood develops some resonance after twenty-five years. On the minus side, twenty-five-year-old strings weren't doing anyone any good. This was before digital vibration tuners, so I was trying to tune with a tone and an untrained ear. Yikes.

Nobody showed up. I didn't give up. I just posted the meeting each week, week after week. I figured I'd use the time to quietly practice while I was sitting there. For the first few weeks, nobody showed.

And then they came out of the woodwork. Phil Morris, who now builds Spanky banjo-ukuleles in Garland, was among this early group of players. Our numbers quickly grew. We would gather at the coffee shop, play folk music we had created with our little chord charts and had in notebooks in a box for people to grab. We didn't keep good records back then, so I'm going to guess we were at about twenty players going strong.

Dallas Ukulele Headquarters members perform at the 2006 Poetry Music Festival. *Photograph courtesy of Dallas Ukulele Headquarters.*

Logan Dafron, who crafted a ukulele for Edie Brickell, was part of that early group, as well.

Then disaster struck—well, a minor disaster, I guess. We got kicked out of the Half Price Books coffee shop for playing too loud. I was actually kind of proud of getting the boot for that reason.[136]

So, where did this band of rowdy ukulele players meet after being kicked out of Half Price Books?

We moved around a little. I remember meeting at the White Rock Lake Yacht Club. Noel Tardy had her Uke Lady Music Store in Lake Highlands Village, and there was a bar and restaurant there. As I recall, sometimes we'd head over to the restaurant, which I think is still there, called Alfonso's Italian Restaurant, according to Google. The bar appears to have gone through quite a few changes. The name now is District 9 Draught Haus. I can't remember the name back then. We would play in the corner of the bar and bring a box of notebooks that had our songs in them. Another member from those days was Katsu Nakayama. Back in those days, the only players who really came through were Pops Bayless and Lil Rev. When Lil Rev was there, he had taught us to roll the ukes by grabbing the bottom under the sound hole and pulling up to spin the uke while we balanced the neck in the other hand as the instrument rotated. Very showy, and fairly easy. Anyway, I have a vivid memory of Katsu and I playing next to each other in this bar, performing this spin, and somehow smacking the body of our two ukes together fairly hard.

—*Mark Levine*

Mark shed some light on where the name Dallas Ukulele Headquarters came from. He gives credit to Austin-based ukulele instructor Pops Bayless, "[Pops] actually gave Dallas Ukulele Headquarters its name. We were down there to watch him and his band Shorty Long perform, and I gave him a list of names we had come up with. DUH is the one he selected."[137]

The growth of Dallas Ukulele Headquarters allowed Mak Levine to bring many well-known ukulele musicians to North Texas. A literal who's who of ukulele stars have given concerts and hands on workshops to Dallas Ukulele Headquarters members and friends. The four-string phenoms who have shared their talents include Kevin Carroll, Mark Baker, David Hendley, Danielle Ate the Sandwich, Stuart Fuchs, Lil' Rev, Kimo Hussey and Jack N Jel (Mark Jackson and Jane Jelbart from Newcastle, Australia).

Dallas Ukulele Headquarters 2011 Memorial Day Jam. *Photograph courtesy of Dallas Ukulele Headquarters.*

DUH has continued to grow and has built a strong ukulele community in North Texas. As Mark says,

> *We meet a couple of times a month. Locations vary, but it is usually a restaurant with a time provided for a meal, for those who want to eat. We jam for about two hours or more depending on the venue.*
>
> *Come and meet other local Ukulele players for our "themed" jam sessions! It's always a BLAST! Should you like to perform, we also have opportunities for our players to come and perform for children, seniors, churches, temples and other appreciative groups!*[138]

The themed jams have included jams for Mardi Gras, St. Patrick's Day, the Fourth of July, Halloween and Christmas. The format allows absolute beginners to feel comfortable, improve and learn from some of the more experienced players.

One of the groups that grew out of the Dallas Ukulele Headquarters jams is the Happy Hour Ukulele Ensemble. In Richardson, Texas, the Four Bullets Brewery opened in May 2015. It wasn't long before the Happy Hour

Dallas Ukulele Headquarters 2014 Concert and Workshop Series

For more information and updates visit our site http://duhukeconcerts.org

The Love Leighs

Feb. 22

Manitoba Hal

Mar. 22

This Event produced by Uke Lady Music.
Times, price, and venues may vary.
See http://lonestarukefest.com/ for details.

Kathy Murray and The Killowats

Apr. 26

Del Ray

May. 31

For Each Event

Concert $15
Workshop $15
or Both $25

Kevin Carroll

Aug. 16

Workshops 4:00 p.m.
Concerts 7:30 p.m.

Pops Bayless

Sept. 27

Join Us At

600 E. Sandy Lake Rd. #106
Coppell, Texas 75019

Cary Cooper

Oct. 11

Register To Attend at http://www.meetup.com/ukulele-84/

Dallas Ukulele Headquarters Concert and Workshop Series, 2014. *Photograph courtesy of Dallas Ukulele Headquarters.*

Ukulele Ensemble became one of the venue's regular performers. The band is composed of longtime DUH members Don Aspromonte, Richard Delcamp and David Harbaugh.

This is the old-school gang! Members are among the oldest members of Dallas Ukulele Headquarters. I played with Don in our duo The Douboys at senior living centers and retirement homes throughout the area. Along with David Harbaugh, Richard Delcamp and a host of talented musicians, the Happy Hour Ukulele Ensemble continues to make great music, and I'm thrilled to call them friends.[139]

Before the Happy Hour Ukulele Ensemble, there were many ukulele players who wanted to perform in public; they became known as the Community Ukulele Band (CUBs). As Mark explains, the group started out under the Dallas Ukulele Headquarters name.

In the old days, we used to have a more active performance element that wasn't branded as DUH CUBs: It was just DUH. We used to have some of our jams at retirement homes and senior centers, so members would just jam, but residents could enjoy the performance, too. There was also a period of time when those senior center performances were done by a little smaller group with some attempt at uniforms: white shirts, bow ties, that sort of thing.

There's also a tie-in with Ebby Haliday: she played the ukulele when she was alive. I mean, obviously, but who knows, maybe she's still playing somewhere. Anyway, her favorite song was the Tony Orlando and Dawn tune "Tie a Yellow Ribbon 'Round the Old Oak Tree." For several years, really up until she passed, Dallas Ukulele Headquarters participated in her birthday events. One year, we played at the entry of the Adolphus hotel (I think) as guests arrived. Another year, she actually had Tony Orlando perform, and we were able to perform on stage either before or after him— likely before. They even arranged a "green room" for us for that event. This was all done under Dallas Ukulele Headquarters, not DUH CUBs.

We've also periodically been asked to perform on WFAA. Most of these were set up by Noel Tardy, promoting the uke festivals.

There's always been a performance element to DUH—really, part of our mission statement. We just have a sort of separate unit for it now.[140]

The highlight for these players is the CUBs Christmas Tour. Through the years, they have played at events and venues such as the Dallas Zoo,

The Dallas Ukulele Headquarters Community Ukulele Band (DUH CUBS) on their 2013 Christmas tour. *Photograph courtesy of Dallas Ukulele Headquarters.*

The Dallas Ukulele Headquarters Community Ukulele Band rehearse for their 2018 Christmas tour. *Photograph courtesy of Dallas Ukulele Headquarters.*

Grapevine Library, Dickens Downtown in Plano, Dallas Heritage Village Candlelight and many others.

The band has also been able to perform shows throughout the years for a diverse range of groups. Mark Levine talked about one of those shows from 2011.

> *It was several years ago that I made the acquaintance of Margaret Wilton. A spunky senior living out at Lewisville Estates, she was avidly interested in all things musical, and especially passionate about the ukulele. She pestered me to come out and give her lessons. She pestered me to bring our group out to Lewisville Estates. She pestered me to help her find rides to Dallas Ukulele Headquarters events.*
>
> *In short, she was a complete joy.*
>
> *Today, I wish we had gone out to play at Lewisville Estates more. Today, I wish somehow we'd been able to arrange more rides for her to DUH events. Not that it slowed her down at all: She formed her own ukulele club at Lewisville Estates, and also taught people how to play just about any instrument you could think of. She did anything she could think of to be an active, vibrant part of the community.*
>
> *When she developed health problems and moved to a smaller facility, The Sterling House, she was again instrumental in bringing my band, The Douboys, to perform. And again, she'd developed quite a following.[141] She was teaching the Executive Director to play Dobro, and his wife to play ukulele. She painted bird feeders. We always looked forward to playing there.*
>
> *Today, unfortunately, I was unable to see Margaret Wilton. She passed away, peacefully, in her sleep, two days ago. Instead of playing our concert today for Margaret, we played in her honor.*
>
> *The music was rich, our audience was involved and engaged, and the show was great. Perhaps Margaret was hovering about for one last show, influencing our fingers and our voices. It was a glorious send off.*
>
> *And today, it doesn't matter what I wished for: She is gone. But I do have one more wish. I wish every senior I encounter was as spunky and persistent as Margaret. If that wish comes true, the world will be filled with beautiful music.*
>
> *So long, Margaret. Safe travels. And God help whomever you ask for a ukulele if all they have is a harp.[142]*

Since 1998, Dallas Ukulele Headquarters have brought "ukulele joy" to thousands of people across North Texas.

Kanikapila and the Opihi Gang

Two Groups Who Are Bringing the Aloha Spirit to North Texas

THE KANIKAPILA ISLAND STRUMMERS

In 2018, Nathan B. Kruse, associate professor of music at Case Western Reserve University, published an article about a North Texas ukulele club.

> *To examine the musical and cultural underpinnings of the Kanikapila Island Strummers, a community ukulele group that celebrates Hawaiian ethos through music and dance. Specifically, this research underscored the Kanikapila Island Strummers' musical practices, the narratives of Hawaiian culture as expressed by club members, and the members' perceived sense of responsibility in preserving and disseminating Hawaiian customs in the Continental United States…Hawaiians' connection to and separation from the islands, and acculturation processes on the mainland. While Hawaiian cultural elements have engendered a rich community of practice, Hawaiian history and sovereignty initiatives remain key aspects among participants. Implications include viewing the "ukulele as a serious instrument that is as much about a people and a place as it is about music."*[143]

The Kanikapila Strummers, in North Texas, was founded by Richard Muir and Obed Donlin in October 2010. Richard remembers,

After bugging Mark about Hawaiian songs, he gave me permission to start the group.[144] I recruited Obed for the songs. We started with three Hawaiian songs and three hapahoui songs and started the songbook. I found a tiki bar in Richardson, "Soul Fish." We picked a day not to interfere with Mark's events or other sporting events. We decided to meet once a month on a slow night for the restaurant.[145]

Richard picked up the ukulele in 2007. He was inspired by his wife, who wanted to learn hula dancing. Richard joined Dallas Ukulele Headquarters, but they did not play any Hawaiian songs. Obed was an obvious leader of the new Hawaiian music group.

Obed Donlin is such a gentle man. I remember discussing the beginning of Kanikapila with Richard Muir, who definitely didn't want to lead it. He "nominated" Obed, who turned out to be amazing. Not just a gentle leader, but a great performer and an excellent resource for all things Hawaiian. He produced so much music for the group that there are at least two huge songbooks. Sometimes, the reluctant leader is the strongest leader. Certainly true with Obed!"[146]

—Mark Levine

Since I was born and raised Hawaiian in Hawaii, I naturally picked up the ukulele and learned it at an early age. I went to rock concerts in high school and played music with high school classmates. Later, I fooled around with the guitar and piano. I also played organ for a rock band. My rock band was The Weeping Willows. It was 1966, 1967, and we played at high school dances and fraternity all night parties at the University of Hawaii. I was inspired to play the ukulele because everyone else was playing it, because it was so simple to learn and play.[147]

—Obed Donlin

Obed moved to Texas on January 15, 2010. He met Richard at a Hawaiian movie that was playing at the Angelika Theater in Dallas Texas. Obed elaborates on the Kanikapila experience.

Kanikapila sessions are relaxing and informal. The songs and chords are easy, and we try to make everyone comfortable by welcoming everyone to come and share the aloha, just like one big happy family! Kanikapila is the best way to share the Hawaiian culture because it's the easiest way, and everyone likes to sing and play the ukulele.[148]

Above: Obed Donlin (*left*) and Richard Muir (*right*), the founders of the Kanikapila Island Strummers. *Photograph courtesy of Dallas Ukulele Headquarters.*

Left: Obed Donlin (*center, rear*) in one of his early rock bands in Hawaii. *Photograph courtesy of Obed Donlin.*

Blowing the conch shells at Kanikapila. The conch shells are always blown at the opening of Kanikapila. *Photograph from the Jeff Campbell collection.*

(*Left to right*) Richard Muir, Uncle Wayne Kahanu and Obed Donlin lead Kanikapila. *Photograph from the Jeff Campbell collection.*

We hold Kanikapila at a restaurant because it's supposed to be a party, much like having it at a luau. It's not really a class or even just entertainment. Kanikapila is where you go to play music, sing songs, eat, drink and have a good time. It helps the atmosphere of sharing the aloha. It's done better at a buffet because you can eat the whole time you're sharing the aloha with friends and family.[149]

Linda Lasseter is a longtime member of the Kanikapila Island Strummers. Linda's mother gave her a Harmony ukulele in high school from "Santa." The Harmony ukulele is a very valuable instrument that Linda still owns. Linda also played guitar in a college band. They played at campus parties and also participated in a local "Up with People" event.

A client left my house to go to Kanikapila, so a month or so later, I asked her about it. She printed out all the songs for me. Richard Muir welcomed me the first time I came. The great thing about all ukulele jams is that everyone is nice and welcoming. There is a range of abilities, and no one judges anyone's playing or singing. People should know that if considering attending. "Everyone starts from the step they are on," which holds true to everything in life.[150]

Good times at Kanikapila! *Photograph courtesy of Dallas Ukulele Headquarters.*

Like most everyone involved in Kanikapila, Linda helps new players "climb the steps."

> *I have helped people when I walk past and notice they are twanging the strings or something. I've shared the couple of chord hacks I know about. I also have told some newbies to skip hard chords and just keep up with the song—then they can participate…also to practice chords during commercials when they are watching TV. I also show them they can play actual songs the first time they pick up a uke…several songs that have C as the only chord. Then they can progress to "Margaritaville"—ha! (That song is 95 percent in C!)*[151]

The songbook that Richard started had 6 songs; it now contains over 150 Hawaiian tunes. In addition, the group now has over two hundred members.

Kanikapila allows native Hawaiians to share the aloha spirit across North Texas.

THE OPIHI GANG

The Opihi Gang is a North Texas Hawaiian band that takes their name from the song "Opihi Man." Opihi is a Hawaiian delicacy. The Opihi is a limpid and referred to as the fish of death or the delicacy of death.

The opihi vigorously clings to the ocean's battered rocks for self-preservation, as they prevent the opihi from being swept away by vigorous waves or predators. Opihi pickers risk broken bones, drowning, immobility from injury or becoming lost at sea in pursuit of this delicacy.

> *Sounds like thunder, gotta head for the high ground*
> *White water coming, no foolin' around*
> *Opihi man in the sun. Opihi man grab your bag and run*
> *Opihi man another swell is coming your way*
> *Opihi man another swell is coming your way*
>
> *Gotta fill up your bag, with the yellow and black*
> *Keep your eye on the wave, don't ever turn your back*
> *Opihi man in the sun. Opihi man grab your bag and run*
> *Opihi man another swell is coming your way*
> *Opihi man another swell is coming your way*

The Opihi Gang perform at the Plano AsiaFest (*top, 2022; bottom, 2023*). *Photographs from the Jeff Campbell collection.*

Like the crab on the rock, you gotta run real fast
Keep your eye on the wave, don't ever turn your back
Opihi man in the sun. Opihi man grab your bag and run
Opihi man another swell is coming your way
Opihi man another swell is coming your way

—lyrics to the song "Opihi Man," written by the Ka'au Crater Boys[152]

In 2013, Richard Muir of the Kanikapila Strummers and Dallas Ukulele Headquarters was invited to jam with a group of native Hawaiians in Garland, Texas. The group started with just a few songs. As they steadily grew, their repertoire increased to have over 160 songs.

By 2014, the group was receiving requests to play at wedding receptions, libraries and other events. They chose to name their group The Opihi Gang. The original band members were Wayne Kahanu on guitar and lead vocals; Kavika Costa and Jay Glowacz on guitar; Tony Kalawe on lead vocals and guitar; and band leader Richard Muir on ukulele.

As of 2024, The Opihi Gang continues to perform with original members Wayne Kahanu, Tony Kalawe, Jay Glowacz and Richard Muir, along with Anna Petschow on ukulele, Wayne's son Ikaika Kahanu on bass and Marvic McElroy playing twelve-string guitar.

23

Keep On Chugging Along

kulele groups love acronyms. For example, there is the Bellingham (Washington) Ukulele Group (BUG), Portland (Oregon) Ukulele Association (PUA) and South Carolina's Predominantly Ukulele Union of the Grand Strand (PUUGS).

Another thing many ukulele groups have in common is the struggle of finding a place to meet. Such is the case with the Fort Worth ukulele group known as CHUG, which, back in the day, stood for Coffee House Ukulele Group (more on that later). Full disclosure, there is also a CHUG group in Chicago and a CHUG group in the UK (the Chorlton Ukulele Group).

The Coffee House Ukulele Group started in 2004. The group met at Artistic Blends Coffee House and Theater on Trail Lake Drive in Fort Worth. The principal organizers were Martha Stookey and Steve Williams. The location, which was originally an old theater, was described by Steve Williams with a bit of wistfulness: "Artistic Blends was just the coolest place!"[153]

Eventually, Artistic Blends went out of business, and CHUG had to find a new place to meet. The group moved around to various pizza parlors and coffeehouses trying to find a home. Eventually, the group moved out to Martha Stookey's lake house on Eagle Mountain Lake, northwest of Fort Worth.

Martha's lake house became quite the beehive of ukulele activity. Mark Levine of Dallas Ukulele Headquarters raved about the location, "Martha's lake house was legendary. We had traveling musicians who came in like Lil

A view of Eagle Mountain Lake
Martha Stookey's lake house.
*Photograph courtesy of Dallas
Ukulele Headquarters.*

Rev and Steve and Amanda Boisen performing as The Barnkickers. Martha used to have a quilting group, and Lil Rev came and did a special quilting show at her house. We also were up there for fireworks on the Fourth of July."[154] Cathy Miller, the "singing quilter," was another artist who performed a house concert at Martha's lake house.

Martha was an active senior citizen, not one to sit in a rocking chair as the days go by. She was a passionate sailor, a member of the Fort Worth Quilt Guild and the Circle 8 Square Dance Club. Martha remained involved in the ukulele community right up until her passing on July 16, 2019, at the age of ninety-two. Once again, the ukulele group was in search of a place to meet.

Fortunately, the First Congregational Church of Fort Worth had started a ukulele group in 2016, the First Congo Ukers. The group first gained attention of the wider ukulele community when they held a workshop with ukulele wizard Stuart Fuchs. The workshop was titled "Beatles Ukulele Immersion, All You Need Is Love and Ukulele." The church provided a gathering place for the Fort Worth ukulele community.

February 23, 2020, would serve as the crescendo for the First Congo Ukers. The ukulele group played with the church band for a Fat Sunday— Let the Good Times Roll concert to celebrate Mardis Gras. The concert featured a Louisiana-centric set list, with songs such as "When the Saints Come Marching In" and "St. James Infirmary."

Then March 2020 happened. The COVID-19 pandemic had an impact on everyone. Many ukulele players shifted to platforms like Zoom or YouTube to get together and play music.

One of the phrases people will use about the pandemic says that "time stood still," but it really didn't. Babies were born, loved ones passed away,

Stuart Fuchs Beatles ukulele workshop at the First Congregational Church of Fort Worth, Texas. *Photograph from the Jeff Campbell collection.*

students graduated from school and folks changed jobs. Such was the case with Lori Dobson.

Lori was on the staff of the First Congregational Church and the main organizer of the First Congo Ukes. She left her position in 2021, and that was the end of the First Congo Ukes. Once again, the Fort Worth ukulele community found themselves without a home. Some would trek over to Dallas (it's farther than you think!) for the Dallas Ukulele Headquarters events.

Then on February 13, 2022, Jim Hannon sent out an email with the message that the Fort Worth ukulele community wanted to hear: "I found a place in the community center that we can use on a Saturday from 11:00 a.m. till 1:00 p.m. free as it will be open to anyone wanting to play the ukulele. The center is next to Southwest High School, not very far from the church we went to. If anyone is interested, contact me."[155]

Veterans of CHUG, the First Congo Ukes, beginning players and other ukulele strummers now had a place in Fort Worth to get together and play. The group now includes some of the Lone Star State's most talented ukulele players, like Jim Hannon, Steve Williams, Tom Steele and Richard Estes.

Jim Hannon is a ukulele enthusiast and has a collection of thirteen ukuleles as of this writing (it will probably be larger by the time you read this). When he is not in Fort Worth, he is probably in Hawaii.

The Fort Worth Fantastic Five (*left to right*): Jeff Campbell, Tom Steele, Steve Williams, Richard Estes and Jim Hannon. *Photograph from the Jeff Campbell collection.*

Steve Williams is a ukulele player and singer who has performed at many venues across North Texas.

Tom Steele is a longtime ukulele player, singer and songwriter. You can find him on YouTube performing his original songs like, "I Could Be Good for You" and "It's Just Kulele Without U."

Richard "Rick" Estes has been playing upright bass since 1961. He is an associate professor of music at the Texas Christian University School of Music. He has performed with the Brazos Chamber Orchestra, the orchestra for the University Christian Church's Boar's Head & Yule Log Festival and the Fort Worth Civic Orchestra.

Richard is also a voice teacher with a forty-year career in opera. He was a Studio Bella Voce instructor at Orchestra Hall during its final year in Fort Worth. Why's a guy like that hanging out with a bunch of ukulele players? "Got my first uke at age 10 (a Roy Smeck). I have a few more by now."[156]

As of 2024, the group still meets at the Southwest Community Center in Fort Worth. The Fort Worth ukulele community keeps on chugging along!

24

Austin Ukulele Society

*I remember when Bob Guz and Jen Richardson were first starting
the Austin Ukulele Society. We've gone down to share jams with them and
performances of groups like the Ukulele Orchestra of Great Britain. They are
always great to work with and one of the best organized groups I've seen.
The musicianship is excellent, and their transition to including virtual when
COVID hit and beyond is wonderful.*
—Mark Levine, founder of Dallas Ukulele Headquarters[157]

ustin, Texas, is known as the music capital of the world. It takes quite an assortment of songwriters, musicians, venues and organizations to earn this title. One of those organizations is the Austin Ukulele Society.

The Austin Ukulele Society (AUS) held their first meeting in January 2011. That first meeting was due to the passion and drive of Jen Richardson and Bob Guz. The Austin Ukulele Society's story begins at a Brooklyn ukulele festival and a live performance on a morning drive radio show in Austin.

Jen is originally from Brooklyn and relocated to Austin in 2006. In Brooklyn, she attended a ukulele festival with an old boyfriend who had an interest in ukulele. Jen had played a little guitar in high school and college but had never pursued music as an endeavor. At the Brooklyn festival, Jen played around with the ukuleles that were being sold by vendors. Finding they suited her small hands, she got one a month later and learned a few songs on YouTube quickly. Soon, she found herself living in Austin.

I was so excited to have something that I could finally learn, and then I went right out to find out who played in Austin and came across Bob's bands. One of the bands Bob played in was called Shorty Long. That's how I got to take some lessons with Bob and Pops Bayless, who founded Shorty Long. That started in about 2007. We've been friends for a long time.[158]

Austin Ukulele Society founders, Bob Guz and Jen Richardson. *Photograph courtesy of the Austin Ukulele Society.*

Bob hails from Massachusetts and went to college in Wisconsin. He moved to Texas in 1981 for graduate school. He thought he would be in Austin for only a few years, but forty-five years later, he's still here.

As a child, Bob played the French horn and trumpet in his school band. In high school, he taught himself how to play guitar, finding joy in singing and playing. Although he was not a music major in college, Bob did take classes in voice and music composition. He also performed in musical productions and a few operas. After college, Bob mainly played guitar in a few bands. He first became aware of the ukulele around 2003.

So, I just happened to be driving to work one day, and they had Shorty Long in the studio, and they were interviewing them, and they played some songs. And I thought, "Oh, this is really cool." They announced as part of the interview that they were going to be playing at a local venue called Flip Genetics that following Sunday, and I was like, "I gotta see this." So, my wife and I went over there, and we watched the band play, and I said to myself, "I gotta be part of this." So, I grabbed Pops during one of the band's breaks and said, "Hey, do you ever give lessons?" And he said, "Yeah, I do." So, I got myself a ukulele and connected with him. A year later, I was playing with the band. Again, it wasn't my first stringed instrument. I found the transition from guitar and adding ukulele pretty straightforward. A lot of it was just learning some of the songs in the repertoire and learning how to do the key changes in the chord changes on the fly, and so, it was a lot of fun. So, I was with Shorty Long probably five or six years. We played at the New York Ukulele Festival. Yeah, it was a lot of fun, and I learned a lot.[159]

Bob also played in another Austin band, the Pine Beetles. The Pine Beetles were an eclectic mix of Celtic music sprinkled with Tin Pan Alley and country songs, with Bob on ukulele! Bob played with the Pine Beetles until 2009.

The year 2010 saw the wheels beginning to turn toward the formation of the Austin Ukulele Society. It was a screening of the film *The Mighty Uke* that revved up the engine. Jen explained:

> *That's part of how we solidified our friendship, I think, is we would bump into each other here and there and jam. There were attempts at having those around town, but they never seemed to really stick or grow. And you know they'd be on a weekend, and then people would get busy and have to cancel them and things like that. Bob's been playing longer, so he may know of some others, but it just didn't seem like any of them really took. Bob and I ran into each other at a showing of* The Mighty Uke. *It was kind of touring around the country, and it was at the Alamo Drafthouse. We ran into each other, and of course we sat together. We were completely blown away, you know; it's such a great documentary.*[160]

Bob added, "Yeah, that was another moment where it's like, 'Oh, man, we gotta do this. We gotta be part of this.' Just seeing *The Mighty Uke* featured a couple of clubs like the Santa Cruz people were featured in that in that movie, but we saw that movie together, that was October 2010."[161]

Bob and Jen had lunch a couple of weeks later to lay out a ukulele group plan. It was decided that Jen would handle the communication, and Bob could kind of lead the group with some songs.

They both felt like other Austin ukulele groups were overly ambitious with a weekly schedule. Bob and Jen decided they would meet once a month. A monthly meeting would be easier for people to commit to, and they have it on the same day and time every month. As of 2024, AUS is entering their fourteenth year. Their meetings have been held on the second Thursday of the month since almost the beginning.

Another key to the Austin Ukulele Society's longevity is a consistent meeting place. Many ukulele clubs struggle to find and keep a regular meeting place. When they started, they met at a local grocery store, Central Market, that has a small classroom in it. As the group grew, the store manager told them they could no longer meet at the store. They were violating the fire code with too many people.

One of the early meetings of the Austin Ukulele Society. *Photograph courtesy of the Austin Ukulele Society.*

One person in the growing ukulele group was also a member of St. John's United Methodist Church. Arrangements were made to meet in a small classroom in the church. Soon, they outgrew that room. There was a divider between that room and another room. So, they eventually removed the divider to double their meeting space. The group continued to grow, so they decided, with church approval, to meet on the church's basketball court.

If you look at some of our older videos, you can actually see some of that evolution. The very earliest videos you'll see are in that little room. Then at some point, we take down the barrier wall, and then at some point, we're in the gym. So actually, it's funny to go back and look at some of our oldest videos on YouTube.[162]

YouTube really helped the club grow in numbers. Bob explained how YouTube became a big part of the Austin Ukulele Society experience.

In 2013 I thought, "Hey, it would be a great idea just to set up a camera and kind of let people see what we're doing here." Because the organization of the meeting is a little bit different than most ukulele clubs that I'm aware of. I have gone to meetings where there's basically a bunch of songs. The idea is to play songs.

I approached, right from the very beginning, that these were going to be more like workshops. Together, Jen and I were going to pick a song, and the purpose of the meeting—or one of the objectives of the meetings—was to teach that song. That is to really do an in-depth analysis of that song, what the strums look like, what the picking parts look like, what the vocals look like, all of that, and then, you know, play it together at the end.

Well, why don't I capture that [on video]? That final performance of what we're doing, plus Jen makes a really good point that that's when our attendance started trending up, because I think it helped people picture [the meeting]. Sometimes, I think it's a little intimidating for people to just walk into a complete unknown situation.[163]

The meetings are accessible for everyone. As the chords of the song are being explained, a one-strum option is given to beginners. So, on a four-beat chord pattern, a player can just strum on the first beat and then get ready for the next chord. For more advanced players, Bob always tries to teach some tab options and some harmonies for those who are more advanced vocalists.

Bob and Jen also want folks to come even if they don't own a ukulele. They can always just sing along with everyone. Most everyone walks away having picked something up. Some learn a new way to play a chord or sing in harmony, new techniques to add to their to their toolkit.

Bob explained, in detail, his teaching philosophy.

The challenge, like in some songs, the strum pattern is something that's tricky, so I want to spend some time on that or a chord progression. What I'm trying to do is figure out in each song again, what are those teachable moments and what are the things that if you learn how to do on this song, you can then take that skill and apply it to other songs?

So again, the idea is to learn that one song, but I try to make it a little more universal, like so that, without people realizing it, by teaching this set of skills, you can actually then go and play a bunch of other songs.

If you're a beginner, here's what you can do, and if you're a more advanced player, here's a different way that you can approach the same thing. Try to do this, and I may show a couple of different tricks. If the song features a particular transition, like, say, a real common one, I touch on is if the song has got a G to an E minor, well, you know, there's at least two different or three different ways you can achieve that transition. Say, you know, if you're a beginner, try this and see if this helps you make that transition more easily. So yeah, I'm looking for teachable moments. I'm kind of presenting this is as, OK, our goal is to shoot a video, but really, that's kind of a tricky thing. I'm using that as a means to be able to teach

The Austin Ukulele Society Ensemble. *Photograph courtesy of the Austin Ukulele Society.*

people different techniques. That's really sort of the underlying goal and the obvious goal is that we want to learn this song well enough to be able to do a really nice performance of it. It just always impresses me. I'm just amazed. People come prepared to work. There's not a lot of fooling around. People show up, and they know we've got a mission, we got a purpose!" [164]

The Austin Ukulele Society also has a performance group, the Austin Ukulele Society Ensemble. Led by Bob, the group has anywhere from ten to twenty ukulele players and one Ubass player. [165] Most of the ensemble have been a part of AUS for a long time, but there are also newer members who participate.

The ensemble plays at local libraries, assisted living facilities, retirement communities and even at an Austin ten-kilometer race that had a stage. Before COVID-19, they performed about once month. After COVID-19, performances have been fewer in number.

Speaking of the COVID-19 era, AUS made a quick pivot as the world began to shut down. Prior to COVID-19, there were 150 to 200 people attending the monthly meetings. AUS was determined to keep the music playing. Throughout the pandemic, AUS began livestreaming their monthly meetings on YouTube. Their YouTube subscribers doubled in 2020 and jumped up another 50 percent in 2021.

Once the pandemic was over and it was safe to meet in person, AUS did not abandon their YouTube contingent. Bob and Jen have maintained a quarterly live meeting on YouTube, in addition to their twelve yearly in-person meetings.

> *It was mostly from popular requests, once it became clear that we were meeting again in person, we just got so many messages from people saying, "Please don't go away; you know keep this going." Well, the request was to continue doing it monthly, and unfortunately for me, that's just not sustainable. But it was like, OK, how about if we do it quarterly? That's basically what we've agreed to do. To do it one once every quarter. There are times where most of the months, our meetings are four weeks apart because we meet on the second Thursday, but once a quarter, it's actually a five-week gap between the second Thursdays, and so that's when we'll host our online streams, when the gap [is] between.*[166]

The quarterly YouTube sessions are fun and informative, but nothing compares to gathering with like-minded ukulele strummers and learning a

When life gives you lemons, make lemonade. The Austin Ukulele Society goes virtual during the pandemic era. *Photograph courtesy of the Austin Ukulele Society.*

A typical gathering at an Austin Ukulele Society meeting. *Photograph courtesy of the Austin Ukulele Society.*

new song together. If you find yourself anywhere near Austin on the second Thursday of the month, please go hang out with the Austin Ukulele Society.

> *It's been a great journey. I had no expectation we would be doing this fourteen years later, nor that we would be having 110 or 120* [members]. *We had one meeting where we had 200 people showed up. It's just astonishing to me, the level of interest. As I mentioned earlier, the level of enthusiasm and dedication that people bring to every one of the meetings. It just blows me away every single month.*[167]

25

Galveston Ukulele Society

In 2017, Professor Robert Krout retired from his position at Southern Methodist University (SMU) in Dallas, Texas. He was a professor of music therapy at SMU's Meadows School of the Arts and had joined the SMU faculty in 2004. Dr. Krout retired as professor emeritus of music therapy. Before retirement, he also taught a ukulele course. The course was offered through SMU Continuing and Professional Education (CAPE). After retirement, Dr. Krout relocated to Galveston Island, Texas, on the Gulf of Mexico.

Why Galveston, of all places?

> When I retired, I really wanted to get back to an island and beach culture and setting. I had moved to Dallas from Wellington, New Zealand, where I lived across from the beach (I was teaching music therapy at a university there). Galveston College was also advertising at the time for someone to teach guitar and ukulele classes, and the Galveston Arts Academy was also looking for the same. So, it was a natural transition for me.[168]

Dr. Krout may have retired from SMU, but he did not idle on the beach in Galveston. He formed the Galveston Ukulele Society, a group that has grown exponentially through the years. GUS has about seventy-five total members on its mailing list, with usually thirty at practices and twenty or so at events.

We started very small, with students from my Galveston College classes. Once I started teaching ukulele courses later that year at OLLI at UTMB Health (Osher Lifelong Learning Institute at the University of Texas Medical Branch at Galveston), many students from those courses joined as well. The group grew quickly, and soon, others joined as well. Setting up our Facebook page and preening in public really helped spread the word.

Robert Krout, the leader of the Galveston Ukuele Society. *Photograph courtesy of Robet Krout.*

GUS receives so many requests for public performance. We try to strike a balance between learning new songs and skills, sharing music and aloha with each other and preparing for and performing in public and for private and community events. We don't want to become just a performing ensemble. We try to limit our performance to about two per month and concentrate on community events, nursing homes and retirement communities and events on the island and nearby. We really enjoy outdoor community events (when it is not too hot). For example, we are featured entertainment next month at the Texas Crab Festival, and later this month, we are providing the live music for the Galveston Oleander Festival.[169]

Dr. Krout also started teaching at the Osher Lifelong Learning Institute at the University of Texas Medical Branch in Galveston. In 2024, four different courses were offered. He is also an adjunct music instructor at Galveston College, teaches Ukulele Bootcamp for www.musictherapyonline. org and performs concerts in the local area. In addition, Dr. Krout operates the website, www.ukuloha.com (Ukuloha—Sharing Aloha Through Music). He has also recorded an album, *Songs from a Music Therapist*, that can be streamed on Spotify and Apple Music.

Dr. Krout has a bachelor's degree in vocal music education from Ithaca College. In addition, the good doctor has three degrees from Columbia University: a master's degree in music therapy, a master of education degree in special education and a doctor of education degree in music education with a focus on music therapy and technology.

The Galveston Ukuele Society's logo poster. *Photograph courtesy of Robet Krout.*

Dr. Krout has also authored the following books: *Therapeutic Guitar: A Powerful Resource for Therapists and Guitar Teachers of Students with Special Learning Needs, Music Therapy Clinical Training Manual, Beginning Rock Guitar for Music Leaders* and *Teaching Basic Guitar Skills to Special Learners*.

> *We continue to welcome new members and look for more opportunities to share aloha through our playing and singing on and off the island. We have great practice facilities at the Recreation Centers and are thankful to the community for their support and interest in having us perform. We are also thrilled to have a sister ukulele group in the Plucking Strummers in Los Angeles. Several of us are traveling to the Los Angeles International Ukulele Festival this year to share aloha and music with them.*

The Galveston Ukuele Society. *Photograph courtesy of Robet Krout.*

We have an awesome leadership team, which has grown as we have evolved. GUS now has three music coleaders, a librarian, secretary, events coordinator and treasurer. We have also added bass and have several folks who play bass on various songs. That really helps round put the sound.[170]

Author's Note: As mentioned in the preface, I was fortunate to be a student in Dr. Krout's ukulele class at Southern Methodist University. He is a patient and encouraging teacher. He is also one of those people who exudes positivity. Galveston is fortunate to have such a talented musician in their community.

26

Joe Stobaugh and the Grace Avenue Ukulele Choir

In 2015, in what I can only describe as urging from the Holy Spirit, I felt this desire to pull my uke out of the case and to practice the uke again. I tend to follow the Holy Spirit's request whenever I can, and so I began to do exactly that, reacquainting myself with the few chords, scales and songs that I knew.

Then, a few nights later, I was surfing around YouTube for stress relief when I came across a performance of the Ukulele Orchestra of Great Britain playing the theme from Shaft *in a live performance. I remember the performance and the leadership of the performance being so delightful and whimsical! I found myself thinking, "I bet I could do this in a sacred context and create an ensemble where we could get music into people and could also have a great time!"*

And thus, the idea was born!

—Joe Stobaugh[171]

Joe Stobaugh is the senior pastor of University Park United Methodist Church in Dallas. In addition, Joe is a multi-instrumentalist, one of those guys who can play about anything he picks up. He has a bachelor of music degree from the University of North Texas, where he studied music education and saxophone, and a master of sacred music degree with a concentration in choral conducting from Southern Methodist University. Joe has released two full-length albums, *Pilgrimage* in 2013 and *Music for Winter* in 2015. Joe also released singles in 2016, 2017 and 2018.

While in graduate school, Joe's professor Dr. C. Michael Hawn encouraged his students to get to know local musicians when they traveled. He said they should immerse themselves in the culture and learn the music of the culture in the places they found themselves.

Joe was able to put Dr. Hawn's words into action on a 2004 trip to Hawaii. After a few days in Hawaii, he purchased a ukulele. Joe introduced himself to a few local musicians and explained what he was doing. The local musicians were very encouraging to Joe on his ukulele journey!

Back in Texas, Joe played a few songs that he had learned and the scales and the chords he had figured out. He would do that once or twice a year from 2004 to 2015 and then he would put the ukulele away.

Joe Stobaugh in a Hawaii ukulele shop. Joe is the founder of the Grace Avenue Ukulele Choir. *Photograph courtesy of Joe Stobaugh.*

> *So, when I experienced the nudge to start the ukulele choir at Grace Avenue United Methodist Church (Frisco, Texas), I wasn't that far ahead of our ensemble regarding my ukulele knowledge and skills. I figured I could learn enough every week to keep ahead of the ensemble in my lesson planning!*[172]

When Joe shared the idea to start a ukulele choir with the church leadership, they were very skeptical. Joe was insistent and was able to persuade church leadership to allow him to continue to develop his idea.

> *I wrote an article about my plan to launch this choir for the church newsletter, and I invited a few people who I thought would be willing and brave enough to try something like this adventure. The first rehearsal was absolutely overwhelming in the response. Within a few weeks, we had fifty people playing! It was incredible the needs the ukulele ensemble was filling for people.*[173]

It wasn't long before the ukulele choir was playing shows, not only locally but also nationwide. The Frisco, Texas–based ensemble performed at the 2016 United Methodist General Conference in Portland, Oregon. An interesting event happened on the way to Portland.

The ensemble took the same flight to Portland with their instruments in tow. A fellow passenger noticed that they were musicians with instruments

The Grace Avenue Ukulele Choir perform at the Frisco Art Walk. *Photograph courtesy of Joe Stobaugh.*

and encouraged them to get up and strum and sing. At thirty thousand feet, they played "When the Saints Go Marching In," and the passengers seemed to really enjoy the impromptu elevated performance.

In 2017, the Grace Avenue Ukulele Choir kicked off their Strumming for Human Rights tour at their home church in Frisco, Texas. The tour continued at Little Rock's Arkansas Children's Hospital, and then the ensemble traveled to Memphis. In Memphis, the group performed at the National Civil Rights Museum and ended the tour with a show at B.B. King's Blues Club on Beale Street.

Joe talked about the challenges of a ukulele band playing in a blues club:

> *The gig…started out a little awkward because the house band was not made aware that we were going to be playing a set that afternoon. And so, they sat at the bar looking at us, and I saw them and made it my mission to win them over in addition to the kitchen staff in the first couple of tunes. So, I played really hard and very intensely to them and the staff, and after the second song, early on into the third, I could see their heads starting to bob and their bodies begin to loosen up a little bit and the kitchen staff grooving in, and I realized we've done it, we'd won the house band over, and that was quite an accomplishment!*[174]

This page: The Grace Avenue Ukulele Choir in Memphis, Tennessee, on their "Strumming for Human Rights" tour performing at B.B. King's Blues Club on Beale Street and at the National Civil Rights Museum. *Photograph courtesy of Joe Stobaugh.*

Performing at B.B. King's Blues Club is a memorable highlight for any musician. However, for Joe, his most memorable show was a Christmas performance at a Frisco mall. For Joe, music is a family affair; his wife, son, daughter, father and father in-law all played in the ukulele choir. The Christmas show was the last time Joe made music with his father-in-law before he died from cancer. As Joe is a cancer survivor himself, the memory is even sweeter.

The year 2020 brought big changes for the ukulele choir. Not only did group rehearsals and performances end due to COVID-19, but Joe was also appointed as the senior pastor of University Park United Methodist Church in Dallas. Like most everyone, Joe and his staff were fighting through each week, trying to innovate their work.

The change in appointment came quickly and unexpectedly. Joe handed leadership of the ukulele choir to Bill Roberts, the associate minister of music at Grace Avenue Methodist. During 2020 and 2021, the group, like many others, met on Zoom.

Once the pandemic era ended, the ukulele choir continued to practice and perform. In 2023, Bill started a new group at Grace Avenue dubbed The Wire Choir. The musical group is for any and everyone who plays a stringed instrument, whether it be a guitar, banjo, ukulele, mandolin, violin, viola, cello, bass, autoharp, lyre, lute, dulcimer, sitar, balalaika, erhu, pipa, guzheng, guqin—you get the idea![175]

As for Joe, the ukulele continues to be a part of his pastoral leadership. In 2024, Joe will be finishing his doctoral degree. He is using the ukulele and inviting people to play it as part of his capstone project for his thesis research.

Joe's thesis is a research question that is posed from an interventionist standpoint. The question is this: Can teaching and spiritual practices about vulnerability help a congregation of predominantly white people exhibit signs of Ubuntu? Joe intends to teach a four-week class around spiritual practices, Ubuntu and vulnerability with longitudinal studies throughout the research.

Ubuntu is a traditional African philosophy. Ubuntu stresses the interdependence of humans on one another. There is a focus on the self's responsibility to others and the world around them. Ubuntu supports the collective over the individual and contends that our society gives human beings their humanity.

Finally, Joe's capstone project will be for the group to learn a few congregational hymns on the ukulele and then perform them in a Sunday morning worship service in front of their peers. If the number one fear among adults in the United States is public speaking, Joe believes that public singing and playing a new instrument would leave one feeling incredibly vulnerable. Joe's hunch is that people will come to really enjoy it, the playing together, the singing together, the fellowship, the music getting into them, and they all want to make more music together.

As Joe says, "Once you've tasted communal music-making with the ukulele, it changes you!"[176]

27

The Ukulele's Mexican Siblings

exas has a Mexican cultural influence. Heck, the very name of the place comes from the Spanish word *tejas*. As you travel around the Lone Star State, you may see a couple of instruments that look like ukuleles. However, a closer look reveals some minor differences.

THE VIHUELA

The vihuela is used in traditional mariachi music, similar in size to a baritone ukulele with a tortoise shell–shaped back. It has five strings and is tuned like the first five strings of a guitar. From low to high, the strings are tuned to A, D, G, B and E. The big difference is that the A, D and G strings are tuned an octave higher than a guitar. This gives the instrument a higher pitch, similar to a tenor guitar. A vihuela is strummed with the fingernails to enhance its sound.

THE JARANA

The jarana is used in son jarocho music, a form of Mexican folk music. The jarana has five courses of eight strings. The first and fifth courses of the jarana are single strings, while the second, third and fourth courses are doubled, similar to the strings on a mandolin. The most common tuning from low to

Left: A member of Mariachi Los Matadores, the Texas Tech University mariachi band, plays a Vihuela at the 2024 Lubbock Arts Festival. *Photograph from the Jeff Campbell collection.*

Below: Three jarana musicians perform at the 2018 Freda Festival in San Antonio, Texas. *Photograph from the Jeff Campbell collection.*

high is G, C, E, A and G. This is very close to the standard ukulele tuning of G, C, E and A.

AS YOU TRAVEL AROUND the Lone Star State, keep an eye out for these instruments, two uniquely Mexican instruments that add so much to Texas culture.

28

The Pandemic Years

The COVID-19 era was a challenge for everyone. Many of us learned that Zoom was not only a verb but also a noun. Ukulele players and other musicians would gather virtually to play and sing. No one expressed this period more eloquently than Barbara Haefeli in the following essay. Her words are also a fitting tribute to an Austin ukulele icon Kevin Jolly.

TUESDAY UKES DURING COVID

A tribute to Kevin Jolly
ukulele evangelist
founder of Tuesday Ukulele Group (TUG)
February 11, 1957–June 14, 2020
by Barbara Haefeli

Tuesday Ukes Members

My apologies to anyone I have inadvertently left off the list.

Paul	Gary G.	Jack	Christine
Marty	Paulette	Miriam	Glenn
Mary Jane	Gary P.	Kent	Brenda
Walter	Fred	Deana	Barbara

Tuesday Ukes website—a good place to find songs! www.tuesdayukes.org

Prologue

The Tuesday Ukulele Group (TUG or "Tuesday Ukes") was started by Kevin Jolly, who passed away on June 14, 2020, during the pandemic at the age of sixty-three. He died of a heart attack. TUG is one of many ukulele groups in this "Music Capital" of Austin, Texas. It provides a community for people to share, enjoy and learn from each other.

Thankfully, the Austin History Center is collecting COVID-19 files where I can, in my own way, honor the memory of Kevin Jolly and those who have kept TUG going strong all this time. The group is meaningful to me as an important element in my week, a mainstay during the pandemic.

Kevin Jolly. *Photograph courtesy of Barbara Haefeli.*

I'm writing this to honor and express gratitude for Kevin, Paul and Marty. Marty and Paul identified a need and a desire for continuity, music and community so have kept it going.

A Night at Tuesday Ukes

It's the day for Tuesday Ukes! I look forward to it.

I carry my music stand from my den, where the piano is, into my study and place it by my computer. Tuesday Ukes meets on Zoom, as does everything else these days. As I set up my music area, I am remembering the days before COVID, when we met at the Hancock Recreation Center. I attend this more regularly than I went to Hancock Center. Now, since it is on Zoom, it no longer requires a drive to Hancock Recreation Center, just a short walk from room to room and some set-up. To fully participate, it also requires preparation of a song.

Preparation of a song, and to participate in the music, means it is necessary to identify a song I want to sing, listen to the new song, practice it and sing it for the group. Many of the songs are "sing-alongs," where the music is displayed while the main person sings. The rest of us sing along. This means that if you do a "sing-along" song, it is best if you find the music and send it to Paul in advance.

I tune my soprano ukulele using a tuner that clips onto the head of the ukulele. I try out each string: G, C, E, A. The C and A strings are sharp, but otherwise, the other strings are in tune.

I sit in a wooden straight-backed, armless chair. Arms on chairs get in the way when I am playing. The wooden chair is just the right height so my feet can be flat on the floor and I can sit up straight.

As I sit in my study, which is actually meant as a bedroom, behind the computer, I look out a window onto my green backyard lawn. It is early evening, so the shadows are lengthening. There is a totally leafed-out pecan tree, because spring is in full swing. The red tip photinia hedge is pruned. The squirrels seem to be in for the day.

My uke is a faithful friend, especially during the pandemic. It eases my mind and my heart and brings me joy and relief from the stress of the day. Plus, it's just plain fun!

I click on the Zoom link. Paul admits me into the Zoom meeting. Others have joined already. More are showing up. We start playing and singing soon after 7:00 p.m. There is not much visiting before we start playing. We all want to play our ukes. Everyone has their ukuleles. Almost everyone has concert ukuleles. They are larger than the soprano ukulele but are tuned the same.

The person who is picked by Paul to play the next song sings, and everyone else mutes themselves. "You're not muted." "You're muted." We smile and chuckle, as this is par for the course for meeting on Zoom.

My pandemic journal is next to me at a table to my left so I can record new information that I learn. A glass of water sits next to me so that between talking and singing, I can sip on it to keep the cracking and creaking of this well-used voice at a minimum.

The song that each person plays is displayed on the screen if it was submitted to Paul ahead of the meeting. The chords are written above the lyrics.

Everyone has their own specialty and their own approach. Mary Jane writes many of her own songs, such as those about the environment. Walter plays the kazoo and, as usual, an old-time song. Mimi often plays an instrumental, as she does this evening. She has a low voice.

Joyfully, my left-hand fingers play the chords, and my right arm strums. I hear the bright ukulele music while singing along with it.

"Barbara, do you have a song?" Paul calls on me next.

I focus on my Zoom screen as I play my ukulele and sing my song of the week for the open-mic portion of Tuesday Ukes. "That's the story of / that's the glory of love." The most common chord progression in the song

"The Glory of Love" is G, Em7, Am7, D7, G. The lyrics and the chords are displayed on the screen as I sing them. The other members of the group are muted and singing along or listening.

Gary and Paulette are next. She has a beautiful, clear voice, and they have prepared carefully. Their elaborate sound system pays off.

We are nearing the end of the open mic. Paul, who has helped keep the meetings going since Kevin died, sings his song next. He does not have his song displayed, so we just listen.

Paul says that since Marty, the other "leader," is not here, he will announce the transition to the happy hour portion. Everyone at Tuesday Ukes tonight understands about it, but when a new person joins, it is explained. Before the pandemic, Tuesday Ukes met at Hancock Recreation Center every Tuesday from 7:00 p.m. until 8:00 p.m. Those who wanted to then headed for the Brewtorium to play some more and have a beverage while doing so. The tradition is carried on this evening through a break in the meeting. Everyone returns with a drink—or at least to visit.

"The meeting will be recorded on the website as usual."

"I got new strings."

"I bought a new uke."

Things are beginning to open up since people are getting their vaccines. Tonight, we talk about Kevin, who started Tuesday Ukes, and how we would like to memorialize him once we meet in person again.

"We could play a video of him and sing along."

"We could get out a songbook he created and sing some of his favorite songs."

It was incredible what he did for us. He kept the group going during the pandemic, and then in June, he died from a heart attack. It is still hard to believe, I think, as the discussion continues.

We all agree how important the group has been for us. Keeping up our ukulele skills. Adding some new members. Learning new songs. Community and caring through music and the ukulele. It is what we have in common and is how we met each other.

"He created so much for us, and then he was gone. UkeAlongs. Senior Sings at Westminster. Loaner Ukes."

"He has been gone since June, but we can still see him in our hearts and minds and on videos."

"We lost our leader in 2020, but we circled the wagons and kept on going."

We all agree that we share a sense of pride at being part of this organic group, Tuesday Ukes.

Epilogue: Kevin J. Jolly Memorial Celebration

For the first time since the beginning of the pandemic, Tuesday Ukes met in person. It will be singing at the celebration of Kevin's life. TUG has chosen songs that were favorites of Kevin's and that he introduced to Tuesday Ukes.

On June 13, 2021, there will be a Memorial Celebration at Catfish Parlour in North Austin. It has taken a year for the pandemic to see the COVID cases declining and enough people vaccinated so that there can be an in-person memorial celebration. It promises to be a celebratory, lively affair filled with gratitude, good food, memories and music.

© Barbara Haefeli, June 6, 2021

ABOUT THE AUTHOR

Barbara Haefeli was born and raised in the Philadelphia, Pennsylvania area. She has spent all of her adult life in Austin, Texas, where she has been playing the ukulele for over ten years. She actually bought and played her first ukulele in the 1970s.

Barbara's first instrument was the violin, which she started playing in the third grade. There was even an elementary school orchestra that she played in. Eventually, her grandfather gave her his violin.

Professionally, Barbara was a systems analyst and instructor. However, she has always enjoyed playing different instruments and singing with various groups for the joy of it. These groups include the Austin Ukulele Society, the Tuesday Ukulele Group, Morningbird, the Austin Choral Union and the Texas State Employees Holiday Choir. These groups have given her the opportunity to lead sing-alongs at the YMCA and retirement communities and to perform at Austin venues.

29

The Next Generation

This book has covered Texas ukulele history from around 1917 until 2024. Ukulele groups like the Austin Ukulele Society and Dallas Ukulele Headquarters will continue to promote the ukulele and support the Texas ukulele community. But who are the young individuals who will take the ukulele in new directions and draw new converts to the little four string instrument? One young, talented Texan is leading the way: Jessica Mauve.

Jessica is an amazing musician, another part of the new generation of musicians. She is both striking out on her own and participating in some of Dallas ukulele Headquarters events. She's a joy to watch.
—Mark Levine, founder of Dallas Ukulele Headquarters

Jessica Mauve was born in the Garden State, New Jersey. Her family moved to Texas when she was six years old. Music is one the ties that bind her family together. Her father is a singer-songwriter and plays many instruments, and the guitar is his go-to when he is performing. Her brother is a singer as well and has made the All-State Choir three times in high school. Jessica's husband plays the drums, and her mother is a dancer.

Jessica's first musical instrument was the piano. However, a dusty, cheap ukulele would take her musicianship in another direction. Her father had bought the ukulele online, and it sat next to their drum kit collecting dust for at least a year after he bought it and tried it out.

> *I finally picked it up (mostly to dust it off) and started learning from YouTube, and after a day of my dad hearing me, he bought a much better one. I am forever grateful for his musical influence in my life. I've never put down the ukulele since! I think I was fifteen when that all happened.*

Jessica has performed in choirs, orchestras, coffee shops, open mics and bars all her life. In July 2023, she decided to take the plunge into performing and producing full time, quitting her day job. "But I only decided recently [July 2023] to quit my job and pursue performing and producing full time." The change had an impact on her income, but it helped that there were a plethora of musical events leading up to her decision. Winning several music and ukulele contests convinced her she made the right decision.

Jessica is also a singer-songwriter! She made her first song when she was four years old. Jessica and her brother were messing around with their father's piano, playing "Twinkle, Twinkle Little Star" and remixing the tune and the lyrics. She has written so many songs since then that she is now recording in her home studio, after years of recording them on live videos, phone voice memos or using her memory.

In addition to being a singer-songwriter and performing artist, Jessica is also a music teacher. Jessica discussed the similarities and differences in teaching and performing.

> *The main difference I see is that although both are similar in many ways, teaching is more about knowledge from music theory and books, while performing is about being in the moment after all that practice. Performing is like "showing" and teaching is like "telling." Maybe my definitions will change as I experience more and more things and teach more people. I draw from my experiences as a performer when I teach, but most things that a student is learning from me is so they can read and express music on their own. I feel that in order to be a great performer, you should also be a life-long learner. You need to constantly teach yourself in order to be the best you can be on stage.*

Dance is also an important part of Jessica's art. Jessica and her mom, Jean, have formed Hulalele, a ukulele and hula group. Hulalele is a play on the words *hula* and *ukulele*. Jean is a wonderful dancer and loves to hula dance, line dance and everything in between. Jean originally wanted to take dance lessons as a child but never got the chance. She began taking lessons less than a decade ago and quit after a year or two due to a cancer diagnosis.

Dance is a major component of Jessica's art. *Photograph courtesy of Jessica Mauve.*

After the challenge of cancer, she continues to dance, and Jessica includes her on some of her shows, so she has more opportunities to perform.

So, what does 2024 and beyond hold in store for Jessica?

> *I am currently self-producing my first music album, which should have been started years ago! Better late than never, though! I was supposed to have the album out last year, but I worked with a "friend" who wanted to produce it, and he totally scammed me. I am now doing the music production side totally on my own and it's been a JOURNEY FOR SURE! I had to start from ground zero and learn all things related to*

sound, what software to use, how to use them, what kind of mics and cables to utilize, how to set everything up, etc. To some, this is probably second nature, but I've taught myself everything I know from the past several months. I have YEARS of performance experience as a choir singer, orchestra player, and now "ukulele artist" but had barely anything on music production. I am in the full throws of this new path in life, and I'm going to keep going and growing. For the future, I plan to share the stage with other uke artists and perform all over the world![177]

Sheet music to "Happy Trails." *From* Daily Ukulele, *by Jim Beloff and Liz Beloff (Milwaukee, WI: Hal Leonard, 2010).*

Happy Trails!

The Chordbusters Ukulele Band always closes their concerts with the song "Happy Trails," made famous by Roy Rogers and Dale Evans. So, "Happy Trails" to you until we meet at a ukulele jam somewhere down in Texas!

Notes

Aloha Texas

1. Reprinted with the permission of David Hendley.

Chapter 2

2. *Fort Worth Star Telegram*, May 29, 1917, www.newspapers.com.
3. *San Antonio Evening News*, August 28, 1922, www.newspapers.com.
4. Classifieds, *San Antonio Evening News*, February 18, 1922, www. newspapers.com.
5. *Brownsville Herald*, October 1, 1922, www.newspapers.com.
6. *Longview News Journal*, February 13, 1926, www.newspapers.com.
7. Jim Tranquada and John King, *The Ukulele: A History* (Honolulu: University of Hawai'i Press, 2012), 118.
8. *Galveston Daily News*, May 8, 1926, 5, www.newspapers.com.
9. *Lubbock Morning Avalanche*, August 8, 1930, www.newspapers.com.
10. *Amarillo Daily News*, February 1, 1951, www.newspapers.com.
11. *Mexia Daily News*, December 10, 1957, www.newspapers.com.
12. *The Call*, March 31, 1961, 14, www.proquest.com.
13. *Baytown Sun*, August 22, 1963, www.newspapers.com.

Chapter 3

14. *Austin American Statesman*, March 31, 1916, www.newspapers.com.

15. *Waco Times Herald*, April 2, 1916, www.newspapers.com.

16. Joel S. Franks, *The Barnstorming Hawaiian Travelers: A Multiethnic Baseball Team Tours the Mainland, 1912–1916* (Jefferson, NC: McFarland, 2012).

17. Baseball's Greatest Sacrifice, "Apau Kau," www.baseballsgreatestsacrifice.com. Gary Bedingfield remembers baseball players who made the ultimate sacrifice for their country.

18. Ibid.

19. *El Paso Herald*, October 14, 1916, www.newspapers.com.

20. *Fort Worth Star Telegram*, March 30, 1916, www.newspapers.com.

21. Ibid.

22. *El Paso Herald*, December 12, 1916, www.newspapers.com.

Chapter 5

23. The term we know as *bluegrass*, as in bluegrass music, originated in the 1940s. Kentucky's (the Bluegrass State) Bill Monroe created a sound so different from country and folk music that it was given its own name. The name came from his band The Blue Grass Boys.

24. Joanna Ray Zattiero, "One Small Girl, a Whole Quartet: Singer/Songwriter Lee Morse" (master's thesis, University of Idaho, 2007).

Chapter 6

25. "Radio Guide," *Radio Guide*, October 11, 1934.

26. Minerd.com, "Frank Wayne Hershaw Jr. (1915–1995)," https://www.minerd.com/bio-hanshaw,_frankwfowler.htm.

27. *Merriam-Webster*, "vaudeville (noun)," https://www.merriam-webster.com/dictionary/vaudeville. In the fifteenth century, several amusing songs became popular across France. These songs were said to have been written by a man named Olivier Basselin, who lived in the valley of the River Vire in northwest France. The songs eventually became known as *chansons de vau-de-Vire*, meaning "songs of the valley of Vire." Other people began writing and performing similar songs, and as this form of entertainment became more widespread, the link to vau-de-Vire was

forgotten. The nickname was shortened to one word, *vaudevire*. As the phenomenon spread beyond France, further changes in pronunciation and spelling shifted *vaudevire* into *vaudeville*. The meaning also broadened to include humorous performances and variety shows.

28. *Travalanche*, "Uke Henshaw: Master of His Instrument," January 13, 2017, https://travsd.wordpress.com/2017/01/13/stars-of-vaudeville-1020-uke-henshaw/.

29. Sandor Nagyszalanczy, "Signature Ukuleles of the Stars of the 1920s and '30s," *Ukulele*, no. 40 (Spring 2023), https://ukulelemagazine.com/stories/signature-ukuleles-of-the-stars-of-the-1920s-and-30s.

30. *Travalanche*, "Uke Henshaw."

31. Minderd.com, "Bobby 'Uke' Henshaw: a.k.a. Charles Robert Henshaw (1896–1969)," https://www.minerd.com/bio-henshaw,_bobbyuke.htm.

32. Minderd.com, "Bobby 'Uke' Henshaw Artifacts," https://www.minerd.com/ukeartifacts.htm.

33. Jake Wildwood & Co., "Bobby Henshaw Baritone Ukulele," October 29, 2014, https://jakewildwood.blogspot.com/2014/10/1950s-sorkin-made-bobby-henshaw.html.

34. A tenor guitar is a four-string instrument.

35. Cinema Treasures, "Trinity Theater," https://cinematreasures.org/theaters/27110.

36. Paul Buskirk would develop a lifelong friendship with Willie Nelson. Nelson would produce and play guitar on Buskirk's 1993 album *Nacogdoches Waltz*.

37. Emando.com, "Paul Buskirk," https://www.emando.com/players/Buskirk.htm.

38. Minderd.com, "Bobby 'Uke' Henshaw."

39. *Cisco Daily Press*, February 23, 1955.

Chapter 7

40. You can read more about the South Palins College bluegrass program in *Texas Bluegrass History: High Lonesome on the High Plains* (Charleston, SC: The History Press, 2021). You can read more about camp bluegrass in *Texas Bluegrass Legacies: Families and Mentors through the Generations* (Charleston, SC: The History Press, 2023).

41. Cynthia McCluskey, *Lubbock Avalanche Journal*, February 26, 1973, www.newspapers.com.

42. Ibid.

43. Ibid.

44. *Lubbock Avalanche Journal*, April 16, 1970, www.newspapers.com.

45. McCluskey, *Lubbock Avalanche Journal*, February 26, 1973.

CHAPTER 8

46. Blesok, "Interview with Johnny Winter," https://blesok.mk/en/sound/reviews-sound/interview-with-johnny-winter-32/.

47. Larry Widen, "Edgar Winter on Playing with His Brother and Creating 'Frankenstein,'" June 29, 2018, https://onmilwaukee.com/articles/edgar-winter-summerfest-interview.

48. *The Johnny Winter Story Blog*, https://bluezzmen.wordpress.com/2018/12/11/johnny-winter-johnny-winter-story-69-76/.

49. Jim and Amy O'Neal, "Living Blues Interview: T-Bone Walker," *Living Blues* (Winter 1972–73, Spring 1973).

50. Texas Music Museum, "Connie Curtis 'Pee Wee' Crayton," https://www.texasmusicmuseum.org/current-exhibits/the-contributions-of-east-austin-african-american-musicians-to-texas-music/blues-music-from-austins-east-side/connie-curtis-pee-wee-crayton.

51. Texas Music Museum, "Major Lee Burkes," https://www.texasmusicmuseum.org/current-exhibits/the-contributions-of-east-austin-african-american-musicians-to-texas-music/blues-music-from-austins-east-side/major-lee-burkes.

CHAPTER 9

52. Justin Martell and Alanna Wray McDonald, *Eternal Troubadour: The Improbable Life of Tiny Tim* (London: Jawbone Press, 2016); Lowell Tarling and Martin Sharp, *Tiny Tim: Tiptoe Through a Lifetime* (N.p.: ETT Imprint, 2022).

53. Ian Whitcomb, *Ukulele Heroes: The Golden Age* (Milwaukee, WI: Hal Leonard Books, 2012), 114–20.

54. *San Antonio Express*, June 23, 1968, www.newspapers.com.

55. *San Antonio Express*, June 25, 1968, www.newspapers.com.

56. Ibid.

57. Ibid.

58. *San Antonio Express*, June 30, 1968, www.newspapers.com.
59. Paula Bosse, "Tiny Tim Mobbed at the Melody Shop—1969," Flashback: Dallas, February 15, 2017, https://flashbackdallas. com/2017/02/15/tiny-tim-mobbed-at-the-melody-shop-1969/.
60. "5,000 Kids Mob Tiny Tim," *Dallas Morning News*, January 24, 1969.
61. University of North Texas Libraries, UNT Digital Library, "WBAP-TV [News Script: Tiny Tim]," June 17, 1969, https://digital.library.unt. edu/ark:/67531/metadc1150243/m1/1/.

Chapter 11

62. Rachel Stone, "Ukulele Lady Noel Tardy," *Advocate*, October 28, 2010, https://lakewood.advocatemag.com/uke-it-up.
63. Gofundme, https://www.gofundme.com/f/SpiritRunners.
64. North Dallas Funeral Home & Cremation Services, https:// northdallasfuneralhome.com/obituary/15248-2.

Chapter 12

65. Horatio Alger Association, "Ebby Halliday," https://horatioalger.org/ members/detail/ebby-halliday/.
66. SMU Libraries, "Ebby Halliday Sings," November 7, 2022, https:// blog.smu.edu/smulibraries/2022/11/07/ebby-halliday-sings/.
67. Ben Tinsley, "Jewish Colleagues Mourn Halliday's Passing," *Texas Jewish Post*, September 24, 2015, https://tjpnews.com/jewish-colleagues-mourn-hallidays-passing.
68. Conner Hammett, "Plano Symphony Launches Revamped Education Program Ebby Halliday Realtors Signs as Two-Year Title Sponsor," *Plano Star Courier*, September 16, 2015, https://starlocalmedia.com/ planocourier/plano-symphony-launches-revamped-education-program/ article_bec50504-5cbb-11e5-873d-57ae01c3e45b.html.

Chapter 13

69. Garret K. Woodward, "Peter Rowan Shares a Timeless Lesson He Learned from Bill Monroe (Part 2 of 2)," The Bluegrass Situation,

September 23, 2022, https://thebluegrasssituation.com/read/peter-rowan-shares-a-timeless-lesson-he-learned-from-bill-monroe-part-2-of-2/.

70. Musicguy247, "Peter Rowan—Bluegrass Artist," October 10, 2014, https://musicguy247.typepad.com/my-blog/peter-rowan-bluegrass/.

71. Peter Rowan Discography, www.peter-rowan.com.

72. Author interview with Peter Rowan, January 7, 2021.

73. Ibid.

74. Ibid.

75. Joseph Terrell, "Defying Expectations: A Conversation with Peter Rowan," The Bluegrass Situation, December 8, 2017, https://thebluegrasssituation.com/read/defying-expectations-a-conversation-with-peter-rowan/.

76. Author interview with Peter Rowan, January 7, 2021.

CHAPTER 14

77. Austin is known as "Bat City." This is due to the 1980 renovation of the Congress Avenue Bridge. The renovation created the perfect bat cave, creating a haven for migrating Mexican free-tailed bats.

78. Michael Barnes, "Kevin Carroll Is the Pied Piper of Ukulele Players Former Roots Rock Guitarist Discovered the Instrument's Spiritual Qualities," *Austin American Statesman*, April 25, 2014.

79. BLOGmaiden, "Review *Ukulele Ceilidh* by Kevin Carroll," *Concert Blog*, April 9, 2019, https://concertblog.wordpress.com/2019/04/09/review-ukulele-ceilidh-by-kevin-carroll.

80. Barnes, "Kevin Carroll Is the Pied Piper."

81. Author interview with Mark Levine, March 28, 2024.

82. Ibid.

83. Ibid.

84. Ibid.

85. Author interview with Mark Levine, March 29, 2024.

86. Author interview with Mark Levine, March 28, 2024.

CHAPTER 15

87. Ibid.
88. Matt Popkin, "Cas Haley: The Talented American," *American Songwriter*, February 7, 2013, https://americansongwriter.com/cas-haley-the-talented-american/.
89. Author interview with Cas Haley, March 28, 2024.

CHAPTER 16

90. Author interview with Mark Levine, April 3, 2024.
91. Dulcimoon, "Dulcimoon Talk #13 - Erin Mae Lewis Talks with Debbie Porter; Live-Streamed 2/16/23," YouTube, July 21, 2023, https://www.youtube.com/watch?v=RyC7pgrycgU.

CHAPTER 17

92. Author interview with Lori Sealy, April 24, 2024.
93. Ibid.
94. Ibid.
95. Ibid.
96. Ibid.

CHAPTER 18

97. Author interview with David "Hambone" Hendley, April 26, 2024.
98. Sam Kemp, "The Life-Changing Moment Tom Petty Discovered The Beatles," *Far Out*, August 20, 2021, https://faroutmagazine.co.uk/the-moment-tom-petty-discovered-the-beatles/.
99. Author interview with David "Hambone" Hendley, April 26, 2024.
100. Ibid.
101. Ibid.
102. Ibid.
103. Ibid.
104. Ibid.

Chapter 19

105. Mike Wilie, "Fort Worth's Premier Ad Man: Frank Burkett Knew How to Work—and Play," *Fort Worth Business Press*, October 5, 2018, https://fortworthbusiness.com/entertainment/fort-worths-premier-ad-man-frank-burkett-knew-how-to-work-and-play/.

106. "Mrs. Burns Uses the Ukulele to Bring Music to Life for 5th Graders," *Abilene ISD News*, May 25, 2019, https://www.abileneisd.org/aisdnews/2019/04/25/mrs-burns-uses-the-ukulele-to-bring-music-to-life-for-5th-graders/.

107. Ibid.

108. *New Braunfels Herald-Zeitung*, May 14, 1995, www.newspapers.com.

109. Richard Gehr, "The Ukulele Is Hot," AARP, April 7, 2011, https://www.aarp.org/entertainment/music/info-04-2011/the-ukulele-is-hot.html.

110. Michael Moschen, "Juggling as Art…and Science," TED2002, March 2002, https://www.ted.com/talks/michael_moschen_juggling_as_art_and_science/transcript?hasSummary=true.

111. "Logan Daffron: From Juggling to Building Ukuleles for Edie Brickell," *Advocate*, July 26, 2017, https://lakehighlands.advocatemag.com/2017/07/26/logan-daffron-juggling-building-ukuleles-edie-brickell/.

112. Gilbert Garcia, "Uke Movement," *San Antonio Current*, July 31, 2003, https://www.sacurrent.com/music/uke-movement-2268157.

113. Arhoolie Foundation, "Adolph Hofner Interview," https://arhoolie.org/adolph-hofner-interview/.

114. Ibid.

115. Damian Lehnis, "John Driskell Hopkins Interview," Kala Brand Music Co., December 11, 2017, https://kalabrand.com/blogs/artist-news/john-driskell-hopkins-interview.

116. "Dallas-Area Men Collaborate on Handmade Banjo Ukes," *Dallas Morning News*, November 23, 2012, https://www.dallasnews.com/arts-entertainment/2012/11/23/dallas-area-men-collaborate-on-handmade-banjo-ukes/.

117. A luthier is a crafter of string instruments such as violins and guitars.

118. Author interview with Lisa "Miz" Markley, February 1, 2024.

119. Album Reviews, "Shinyribs: *Okra Candy*," *Elmore Magazine*, June 26, 2015, www.elmoremagazine.com/2015/06/reviews/albums/shinyribs.

120. Chip Chandler, "Shinyribs' Frontman Gives Insight on Songs," *Amarillo Globe-News*, August 6, 2014, https://www.amarillo.com/story/

entertainment/local/2014/08/06/shinyribs-frontman-gives-insight-songs/13264134007/.

121. Author interview with Washtub Jerry, May 18, 2024.

CHAPTER 20

122. William Yardley, "Martin Sharp, 71, an Artist Who Shaped Imagery of Rock, Dies," *New York Times*, December 5, 2013, https://www.nytimes.com/2013/12/06/arts/design/martin-sharp-71-pop-artist-who-tested-boundaries-dies.html.

123. Bucks Burnett, "Bucks Burnett's Namedropper: How I Met Tiny Tim," *Dallas Observer*, July 7, 2016, https://www.dallasobserver.com/music/bucks-burnetts-namedropper-how-i-met-tiny-tim-8462542.

124. Adam Sheets, "Tiny Tim, Mr. Ed, and Eight-Track Collecting: A Conversation with Bucks Burnett," *No Depression*, February 2, 2011, https://www.nodepression.com/tiny-tim-mr-ed-and-eight-track-collecting-a-conversation-with-bucks-burnett/.

125. Ibid.

126. Ibid.

127. The Bronco Bowl was demolished in 2003, and now, a Home Depot resides on the Fort Worth Avenue site.

128. Lyrics courtesy of Lyrics on Demand, "TV Themes: *Mr. Ed*," https://www.lyricsondemand.com/tvthemes/mredlyrics.html.

129. Danny Gallagher, "How a Fan Club Devoted to a Talking Horse Ended Up Attracting Rock Star Members Like Iggy Pop," *Dallas Observer*, April 26, 2017, https://www.dallasobserver.com/music/this-weird-dallas-fan-club-had-rock-stars-for-members-in-the-70s-and-80s-9403447.

130. Record Store Day, "*One Man Parade: Live from Dallas July 4th, 1994*," https://recordstoreday.com/UPC/616967901603.

131. Danny Gallagher, "Bucks Burnett Recalls Parts of Tiny Tim's Life That Didn't Make the Documentary," *Dallas Observer*, April 26, 2021, https://www.dallasobserver.com/music/what-the-tiny-tim-documentary-left-out-according-to-his-manager-12010628.

132. Terry Gross, "Carl Finch Discusses Working with Tiny Tim," *Fresh Air*, June 17 1996, https://freshairarchive.org/segments/carl-finch-discusses-working-tiny-tim.

133. ALLMUSIC, "'Girl': Brave Combo/Tiny Tim," https://www.allmusic.com/album/girl-mw0000186025.

Chapter 21

134. Author interview with Obed Donlin, October 27, 2023.
135. Author interview with Mark Levine, November 26, 2024.
136. Author interview with Mark Levine, December 5, 2023.
137. Author interview with Mark Levine, March 28, 2024.
138. Dallas Ukulele Headquarters, https://www.meetup.com/ukulele-84/.
139. Author interview with Mark Levine, April 4, 2024.
140. Author interview with Mark Levine, January 23, 2024.
141. The Douboys are a ukulele duo featuring Mark Lavine and Don Aspromonte.
142. *Uke Plucks*, http://ukeplucks.blogspot.com.

Chapter 22

143. Nathan B. Kruse, "The Jumping Flea Diaspora: An Ethnographic Exploration of Music and Culture in a Hawaiian 'Ukulele Club," Taylor & Francis Online, September 6, 2018, 603–15, https://www.tandfonline.com/doi/abs/10.1080/14613808.2018.1516745.
144. Author interview with Richard Muir, October 15, 2023.
145. Ibid.
146. Author interview with Mark Levine, April 4, 2024.
147. Author interview with Obed Donlin, October 27, 2023.
148. Ibid.
149. Author interview with Obed Donlin, March 3, 2023.
150. Author interview with Linda Lassiter, October 4, 2023.
151. Ibid.
152. Obed Kalamaku Donlin and Richard Kupono Muir, *The Kanikapila Island Strummer Songbook* (self-published, 2008), 85.

Chapter 23

153. Author interview with Steve Williams, February 26, 2024.
154. Ibid.
155. Email received by the author from Jim Hannon, February 13, 2022.
156. Flea Market Music Inc., "Player Profile: Richard Estes," https://www.fleamarketmusic.com/directory/player.asp?ID=13083.

Chapter 24

157. Author interview with Mark Levine, April 4, 2024.
158. Author interview with Jen Richardson, April 19, 2024.
159. Author interview with Bob Guz, April 19, 2024.
160. Author interview with Jen Richardson, April 19, 2024.
161. Author interview with Bob Guz, April 19, 2024.
162. Ibid.
163. Ibid.
164. Ibid.
165. A Ubass is a "ukulele bass," basically a small acoustic/electric bass guitar.
166. Author interview with Bob Guz, April 19, 2024.
167. Ibid.

Chapter 25

168. Author interview with Dr. Krout, April 11, 2024.
169. Ibid.
170. Ibid.

Chapter 26

171. Author interview with Joe Stobaugh, May 3, 2024.
172. Ibid.
173. Ibid.
174. Ibid.
175. Email received by the author from Bill Roberts, October 10, 2023.
176. Author interview with Joe Stobaugh, May 3, 2024.

Chapter 29

177. Author interview with Jessica Mauve, April 29, 2024.

About the Author

Jeff Campbell is a writer, musician, electrician, historic preservationist, historian and museum professional.

Jeff has written for *Plano Magazine*, *Turnstyle: The SABR Journal of Baseball Arts*, *The Daily Yonder*, Friends of the Blue Ridge Parkway, Stephen F. Austin State University and Cowboy Poetry at the BAR-D Ranch. He was also the winner of the 2011 Christmas Cowboy Poetry contest (adult division) with the National Cowgirl Museum & Hall of Fame.

He also wrote the book *Murder and Mayhem on the Texas Rails* (The History Press, 2022). And he coauthored *Texas Bluegrass Legacies* (The History Press, 2023), *Plano Past and Present* (The History Press, 2023), *Texas Bluegrass History* (The History Press, 2021), *Hidden History of Plano, Texas* (The History Press, 2020), *Football and Integration in Plano, Texas: Stay in There, Wildcats!* (The History Press, 2014) and *Plano's Historic Cemeteries* (Arcadia Publishing, 2014).

An experienced ukulele player, Jeff has jammed with many of the ukulele groups in Texas. In addition, he plays bass for the Fort Worth Library All Ages Band and ukulele with the Chordbusters Ukulele Band. Jeff has also played bass for the Dallas Ukulele Headquarters Community Ukulele Band and played rhythm guitar with the Opihi Gang.

Visit us at
www.historypress.com